5 Critical Thinking Assignments
Volume 1

Student Version

ALL RIGHTS RESERVED

No part of this book may be reproduced or transmitted in any form or by any means, electronic or mechanical, including photocopying, recording or by any information storage and retrieval system, without permission in writing from K.J. Sukhu.

Copyright © 2013, 2014
K.J. Sukhu

ISBN-13: 978-0993669316
ISBN-10: 099366931X

This is a work of fiction. All names, people, characters, companies, situations, scenarios, places and events are either the products of the author's imagination or used in a fictitious manner. Any resemblance to actual persons, living or dead, or actual events that have occurred is purely coincidental.

CONTENTS

Case Study 1: Building a Balanced Society   CS – 1
    Creating a society with a strong work force while maintaining a healthy environment.

Case Study 2: The Pollution of Lake Okinawa   CS – 2
    Understanding the hazards of manufacturing on the environment and our health.

Case Study 3: The Mysterious Seven of Drewersville   CS – 3
    An investigation using DNA, blood samples, and reports to solve a series of murders.

Case Study 4: The Dolphin Hotel   CS – 4
    A case study in which victims, murderers and accomplices need to be identified using blood samples, DNA and reports.

    (This is an advanced case study lab.)

Case Study 5: The Upper Crescent College Hockey Hazing Trial   CS – 5
    A Court Case: Prosecution vs. Defense

Appendix   A – 1
    Instructional guide for DNA analysis.

Building a Balanced Society

Creating a society with a strong work
force while maintaining a healthy environment

Building a Balanced Society
A Climate Change/Political Lab

K.J. Sukhu

Introduction	It's not always easy to make the best decisions for our environment. Humans know how to heal our world, but yet we rarely do. In this investigation you will explore why maintaining our world whilst balancing society's needs is such a difficult job.
Purpose	To see how our society views the environment and the costs we need to weigh.
Background	Congratulations! You have been sworn in as **the new Mayor** of Azure. However, you only have the position because the current mayor (your old boss) resigned due to a scandal. This means that there will be a new election soon. As the Interim Mayor, you want to hold on to power. The only way to do this is to present a plan to voters that will win enough votes to capture the Mayoral seat.

Your Job as the Interim Mayor Will Be To…

1. **Create a city that has a healthy environment.**
   - Higher environmental ratings positively affect global health.
2. **Create as much employment as possible.**
   - The more jobs created, the higher the standard of life.
3. **Keep the voters happy.**
   - Not enough votes? You will lose the election!
4. **Balance the budget.**
   - Run out of money? You'd better get some more, quickly!

What Choices Will You Make That Ensures Azure is Clean and Prosperous?

You will begin with a budget of $70,000 (or if you want more of a challenge you can start with $50,000). You can purchase any available service on the "Investment" pages. However, you can only purchase an Investment once (i.e. you cannot buy the same Investment multiple times). Also, you may not purchase conflicting Investments (i.e. if you cut funding to the police, you cannot hire police). You must make a minimum of 30 Investments (however, the more Investments you make the more involved you are in city affairs).

Everytime you make an Investment each of the above mentioned categories may be negatively or positively affected. You want all categories to be as high as possible.

In the course of selecting your Investments you may have temporary negative values for your Environmental rating, Jobs created and Votes categories, but you can never have a negative budget at any time.

Building a Balanced Society
A Climate Change/Political Lab

K.J. Sukhu

Example: Let's say (after carefully looking over the different Investments) you decided to "Buy 5 Solar Power Generators" and then for your second Investment you decided to "Increase the Price of Water" (you also decided to start off with a budget of $70,000).

	Investments	Votes	Cost ($)	Environment	Jobs
	STARTING INVESTMENTS	0	70,000	0	0
1	Buy 5 Solar Power Generators	+ 3	− 6,000	+ 6	+ 4
	New Total	+ 3	64,000	+ 6	+ 4
2	Increase the Price of Water	− 5	+ 13,000	+ 4	0
	New Total	− 2	77,000	+ 10	+ 4

After making two Investments, it has resulted in -2 Votes, a revised budget of $77,000, a +10 Environmental rating and you have created +4 Jobs. You still have at least 28 Investments to select and even though the Environment is looking decent the Votes are terrible! In this case, you'll want to get Votes, Environment and Jobs as high as possible. There is no "magic number" you need to reach. The best plan wins, so select your Investments wisely.

Special Rules to Remember!
- Remember, preventing climate change needs to be addressed.
- You **CANNOT** have a **NEGATIVE** budget at any time but all other categories may have negatives.
- You may only select an Investment **ONCE**.
- You may not use conflicting Investments (i.e. if you cut funding to the police, you can't hire police).
- If your addition or subtraction is incorrect you will lose the election (so be careful).
- You must use a **minimum** of 30 Investments (however, the more, the better).
- Your starting budget is: **$70,000** (if you want an advanced difficulty setting start with **$50,000** instead).

*** Do not show other classmates your numbers. Remember, they're competing for the same job as you. If you leak your numbers then your competitors may gain the upperhand! The best proposal will win the job (and only one can win).

Building a Balanced Society
A Climate Change/Political Lab

K.J. Sukhu

Possible Investments for Your Government

	Investments	Votes	Cost ($)	Environment	Jobs
1	Buy 5 Solar Power Generators	+ 3	− 6,000	+ 6	+ 4
2	Extend Coal Power Generating Contracts	+ 15	+ 15,000	− 18	+ 20
3	Pay Schools to Grow Food for Food Bank	+ 5	− 3,000	+ 3	+ 1
4	Allow Pesticide Use to Grow Food	0	− 1,200	− 2	+ 3
5	Pay Companies to Plant Trees	0	− 5,000	+ 6	+ 2
6	Cancel Coal Generating Contracts	− 15	− 15,000	+ 15	− 20
7	Give Tax Break to Businesses	− 5	− 15,000	0	+ 6
8	Give Tax Break to Citizens	+ 10	− 10,000	0	− 10
9	Create a Municipal Compost Program	+ 3	− 5,000	+ 5	+ 2
10	Increase Gas Prices	− 20	+ 20,000	0	0
11	Decrease Gas Prices	+ 20	− 29,000	0	0
12	Buy 100 Wind Turbines	+ 2	− 15,000	+ 5	+ 3
13	Raise Hydro Prices	− 9	+ 6,000	0	0
14	Lower Hydro Prices	+ 1	− 6,000	0	0
15	Introduce a New "Green Tax"	− 55	+ 40,000	+ 25	+ 10
16	Hire Scientists to Study Climate Change	0	− 35,000	+ 20	+ 3
17	Use a Private Company to Study Climate	− 5	− 10,000	+ 5	0
18	Help Subsidize Local Farmers	+ 6	− 4,000	+ 7	+ 2
19	Buy Foreign Food	+ 5	− 2,000	+ 3	0
20	Expand Transportation (Build a Subway System)	+ 11	− 45,000	+ 15	+ 7
21	Cut Funding to Transportation Development Projects	− 4	+ 15,000	− 4	− 3
22	Increase Cost of Using Public Transportation	− 8	+ 12,000	− 4	0
23	Increase Funding to Health Care	+ 4	− 25,000	+ 2	+ 4
24	Decrease Funding to Health Care	− 5	+ 15,000	0	− 3
25	Increase Funding to the Police Department	+ 4	− 15,000	0	+ 3
26	Decrease Funding to the Police Department	− 4	+ 8,000	0	− 5
27	Increase Funding to Education	+ 4	− 18,000	0	+ 5
28	Decrease Funding to Education	− 6	+ 9,000	0	− 4
29	Subsidize Summer Employment for Students	+ 1	− 6,000	0	+ 4
30	Import Goods From Other Countries	+ 7	− 2,000	− 5	− 3
31	Create Goods Locally	+ 6	− 8,000	− 2	+ 6
32	Fix Roads	+ 11	− 10,000	+ 2	+ 4
33	Snow Removal (Using Salt)	+ 12	− 8,500	− 8	+ 2
34	Maintain Parks	+ 2	− 3,000	+ 3	+ 2
35	Use Oil from Tar Sands	− 20	+ 50,000	− 35	+ 10
36	Expand Building Development Project	+ 6	− 15,000	− 8	+ 15
37	Enact Business Pollution Reduction Law	+ 5	+ 10,000	+ 7	− 12

Building a Balanced Society
A Climate Change/Political Lab

K.J. Sukhu

#	Action									
38	Ignore Businesses That Pollute	−	12	−	5,000	−		10	+	15
39	Ban Smoking in Public Places		0	−	17,500	+		11	−	4
40	Help Fund National Parks	+	4	−	8,000	+		8	+	2
41	Increase the Price of Water	−	5	+	13,000	+		4		0
42	Decrease the Price of Water	+	5	−	8,000	−		5		0
43	Deliver City Garbage to Neighboring City	+	4	−	15,000	+		14	−	5
44	Create City Owned Garbage Dump	−	3	−	25,000	+		10	+	12
45	Promote Tourism for the City		0	−	10,000			0	+	7
46	Cut Trees for Paper	−	5	+	12,500	−		7	+	15
47	Hire More Firefighters	+	3	−	8,000	+		3	+	3
48	Cut the Budget for Fire Services	−	3	+	6,000	−		1	−	1
49	Hire Scientists to Study Lake Pollution		0	−	25,000	+		10	+	3
50	Lobby Federal Government for Additional Funds	−	25	+	30,000			0		0
51	Lobby State/Provincial Government for Funds	−	18	+	10,000			0		0
52	Donate Money to Several Charities	+	10	−	5,000			0		0
53	Close Roads to Allow Parades	+	5	−	1,500	−		2	+	2
54	Create a Public Holiday	+	10	−	7,100			0	−	2
55	Hire More EMS Staff	+	2	−	6,700			0	+	3
56	Cut EMS Staff	−	1	+	4,200			0	−	1
57	Give Tax Break for "Energy Friendly" Homes	+	6	−	4,700	+		6	+	2
58	Initiate Garbage Pick Up Services Every 2 Weeks	+	4	−	11,000	+		5	+	2
59	Initiate Garbage Pick Up Services Every Week	+	7	−	22,000	+		2	+	4
60	Increase Property Taxes	−	20	+	25,000			0	−	5
61	Freeze Property Taxes	+	15	−	21,000			0	+	2
62	Increase the Tax on Consumer Goods	−	25	+	25,000			0	+	1
63	Create More Roads & Highways	+	30	−	32,000	−		15	+	9
64	Make "Toll" Highways	−	5	+	12,000	−		9	+	3
65	Mandate Cars Pass an Emission Test	−	2	+	5,000	+		8	+	3
66	Create "Green Eco Tax" on all Electronics	−	4	+	6,100	+		7	+	2
67	Sell City Owned Recycling Plant to Private Business	−	18	+	28,000	−		6	−	4
68	Keep Community Pools Open	+	5	−	7,600	−		1	+	3
69	Close Community Pools	−	5	+	5,000			0	−	4
70	Raise High School Community Service Hours to 80	+	1		0	+		3	−	2
71	Charge Citizens 10 Cents per Grocery Bag	−	3	+	800	+		5		0
72	Make Grocery Bags Free	+	2	−	250	−		3	−	1
73	Increase Funding to Humane Society	−	2	−	2,100	+		3	+	1
74	Decrease Funding to Humane Society	−	4	+	3,000	−		1	−	1
75	Increase the Number of Cell Phone Towers	+	4	−	8,100	−		6	+	3

Building a Balanced Society
A Climate Change/Political Lab

K.J. Sukhu

Tracking Your Investments (Rough Work)

	Investments	Votes	Cost($)	Environment	Jobs
	STARTING INVESTMENTS	**0**		**0**	**0**
1					
	New Total				
2					
	New Total				
3					
	New Total				
4					
	New Total				
5					
	New Total				
6					
	New Total				
7					
	New Total				
8					
	New Total				
9					
	New Total				
10					
	New Total				
11					
	New Total				
12					
	New Total				
13					
	New Total				
14					
	New Total				

IMPORTANT: This report contains proprietary and original material. Accordingly, this document may not be copied or released to third parties without consent.

Building a Balanced Society
A Climate Change/Political Lab

K.J. Sukhu

15					
	New Total				
16					
	New Total				
17					
	New Total				
18					
	New Total				
19					
	New Total				
20					
	New Total				
21					
	New Total				
22					
	New Total				
23					
	New Total				
24					
	New Total				
25					
	New Total				
26					
	New Total				
27					
	New Total				
28					
	New Total				
29					
	New Total				
30					
	New Total				

31					
	New Total				
32					
	New Total				
33					
	New Total				
34					
	New Total				
35					
	New Total				
36					
	New Total				
37					
	New Total				
38					
	New Total				
39					
	New Total				
40					
	New Total				
41					
	New Total				
42					
	New Total				
43					
	New Total				
44					
	New Total				
45					
	New Total				
	FINAL TOTALS				

Building a Balanced Society
A Climate Change/Political Lab

K.J. Sukhu

Tracking Your Investments (Final Copy)

	Investments	Votes	Cost($)	Environment	Jobs
	STARTING INVESTMENTS	0		0	0
1					
	New Total				
2					
	New Total				
3					
	New Total				
4					
	New Total				
5					
	New Total				
6					
	New Total				
7					
	New Total				
8					
	New Total				
9					
	New Total				
10					
	New Total				
11					
	New Total				
12					
	New Total				
13					
	New Total				
14					
	New Total				

IMPORTANT: This report contains proprietary and original material. Accordingly, this document may not be copied or released to third parties without consent.

Building a Balanced Society
A Climate Change/Political Lab

K.J. Sukhu

15					
	New Total				
16					
	New Total				
17					
	New Total				
18					
	New Total				
19					
	New Total				
20					
	New Total				
21					
	New Total				
22					
	New Total				
23					
	New Total				
24					
	New Total				
25					
	New Total				
26					
	New Total				
27					
	New Total				
28					
	New Total				
29					
	New Total				
30					
	New Total				

Building a Balanced Society
A Climate Change/Political Lab

K.J. Sukhu

31					
	New Total				
32					
	New Total				
33					
	New Total				
34					
	New Total				
35					
	New Total				
36					
	New Total				
37					
	New Total				
38					
	New Total				
39					
	New Total				
40					
	New Total				
41					
	New Total				
42					
	New Total				
43					
	New Total				
44					
	New Total				
45					
	New Total				
	FINAL TOTALS				

IMPORTANT: This report contains proprietary and original material. Accordingly, this document may not be copied or released to third parties without consent.

Building a Balanced Society
A Climate Change/Political Lab

K.J. Sukhu

Graphing Your Investment Portfolio

Once you have finished selecting your Investments and have "run the numbers", it's time to represent your Investments graphically.

As you have generated a lot of data with differing categories, you will need to construct a graph with multiple y-axes, labeled y_1 and y_2 (refer to Figure 1-1). On the x-axis you will put the number of your Investments.

You will use the y_1-axis for your "ratings" (Environment, Jobs and Votes). You should notice that the y_1-axis extends down below the "zero" mark because you are allowed to have a negative rating in any of these categories.

You will use the y_2-axis for your budget. You will notice that this axis does not extend below zero, as you were not allowed to hold a negative budget.

Notes for Building Your Graph:
- Each category should be displayed in a different color.
- A legend should be present.
- Titles for all axes and the graph should be well thought out.
- Appropriate scaling should be used for all axes.

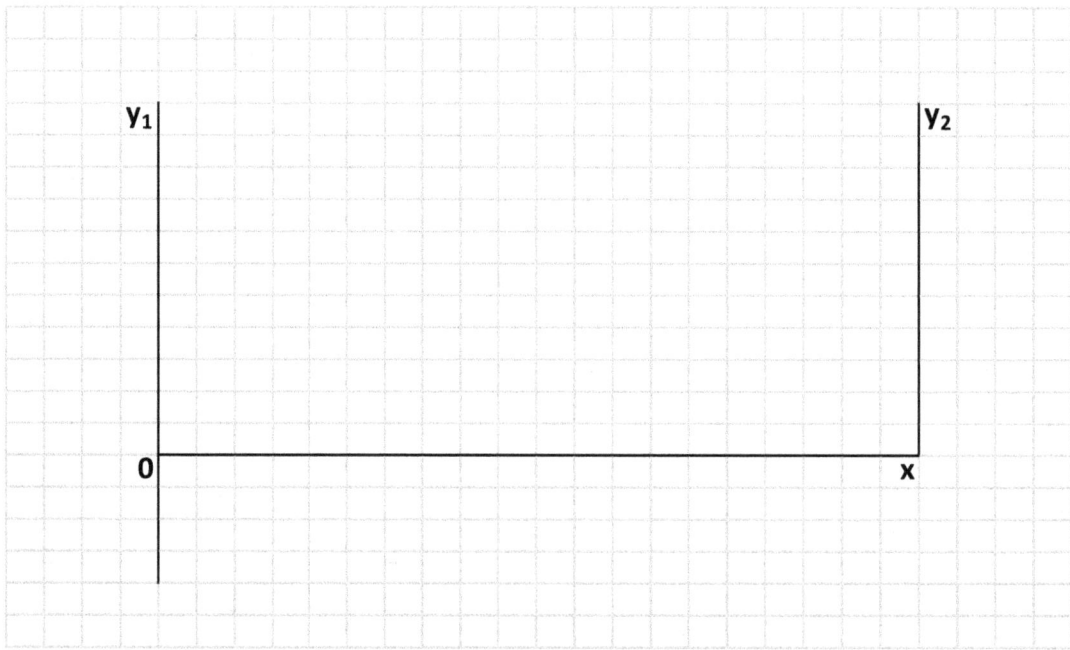

Figure 1-1: Template graph for your portfolio statements.

IMPORTANT: This report contains proprietary and original material. Accordingly, this document may not be copied or released to third parties without consent.

CS1-11

Building a Balanced Society
A Climate Change/Political Lab

K.J. Sukhu

Building a Balanced Society
A Climate Change/Political Lab

K.J. Sukhu

The Pollution of Lake Okinawa

Understanding the hazards of manufacturing
on the environment and our health

The Pollution of Lake Okinawa
An Anthropogenic Lab

K.J. Sukhu

Introduction Science isn't always about producing numbers, but rather, sometimes solving a problem using given data. In this activity you will use the information provided to discover who is poisoning Lake Okinawa.

Background A lake that services the region of New Londo was recently found to be polluted. There are several towns that rely on the drinking water from Lake Okinawa. Several citizens are dead and many more are sick. Initial medical reports indicate that those who died mainly lived in the South-Western area of the lake known as Soel. High levels of mercury were found in the blood of the deceased. Many of the sick were reportedly from the North-Western region known as Jiftar. On the Eastern side of the lake is a community known as Erista which has reported that only 30% of their citizens have reported an illness.

Procedure The police have hit a dead end and would like a scientific explanation of what happened. They have faxed you all the details and have commissioned you to make a report on the following:

- **Who or what is causing the deaths and illness?**
- **Where is the source of the illness?**
- **Why has one third of the population of Erista reported an illness as compared to the entire town of Jiftar?**
- **Who is/are responsible and possible motives?**
- **What is your proof that the other parties are innocent?**

You must also be able to explain small details of the story. In all, you must come up with a **logical explanation** without any holes in your story.

Keep in mind that you will receive some facts, some lies and will have to piece together a logical explanation as to who is responsible and what their motives are. Remember if you get it wrong, there will be severe consequences for the citizens who rely on you.

Note: because you are not there you will have to use the data to put together a detailed visual representation of the town.

In the very North-Eastern part of New Londo lays the industrial district. They mass produce many products for different areas of North America. These factories are believed to be the prime suspects in the pollution of

The Pollution of Lake Okinawa
An Anthropogenic Lab

the lake. One of the factories may be illegally dumping chemicals. Your job is to find out which one is the culprit (if at all).

To Help You Solve the Case You Will Have the Following Information
- Suspects List
- Weather/Meteorological Report
- Official Statements, Background Information and Environmental Assessments of the Companies
- Geographical Landscape
- Other Various Reports Gathered

Suspects List

Xenoware Inc. At this plant, Xenoware Inc. is creating a "next-gen" gaming platform. It mainly deals with metal and plastic components.

Quad Appeal At this plant, Quad Appeal produces shoes and hats. The factory uses a tremendous amount of noxious dyes and adhesive agents.

Infinitysoft The Infinitysoft plant mass produces its second generation "Infinity Starmap" nicknamed "Infinity-star". These devices play music and videos in a small, easy-to-carry device. The plant handles a large quantity of metallic and plastic components.

Presidium Green This factory is used to create "Green-River" players and high resolution TVs. The plant uses a large number of metallic and plastic components.

Stasis Tech Stasis Tech uses their factory to create its "Solaris" smartphone. It uses a relatively small amount of metallic and plastic components.

Weather/Meterological Report

A meteorologist has confirmed the weather was "unusual" directly prior to the first incidents of people reporting their illnesses. Her reports indicate that, two weeks prior to the first reported illness, there was a "tremendous amount of rain". This rainfall lasted for about a week. After that, the town experienced a heat wave for a few days. Finally, two days before the first reported illness, the town experienced heavy rainfall yet again. It was also stated that winds routinely come from the North.

The Pollution of Lake Okinawa
An Anthropogenic Lab

K.J. Sukhu

Official Statements, Background Information and Environmental Assessments of the Companies

Xenoware Inc.

Official Statement:

"We at Xenoware are saddened by the deaths of the individuals. However, in no way are we responsible for the environmental destruction of the lake. We are vigilant when it comes to our operations and we can ensure that our customers receive the highest quality products while protecting our environment. Why would we risk our reputation? It is what drives our business and we have had record profits over the last few years."

Background Information:

5 years ago Xenoware Inc. was accused of releasing a sub-par gaming machine that was prone to break. This was dubbed the "Orange Orb of Death" (OOD). It was later rumored that the company knew the systems were faulty but rushed it to market in order to gain an edge over its competitors. These allegations however, have never been substantiated. Many people needed to replace their defective consoles which resulted in increased profits for Xenoware. Xenoware also released the "Fever High", a portable multimedia player. This device also had hardware issues and was prone to freeze. The company makes most of its profit from its software division as opposed to its gaming division.

Environmental Assessment:

The factory in question mainly deals with metal and plastic components. This plant employs 12,000 workers. They are creating the "Xenobox-Rouge". It is estimated that the plant is creating 2 million consoles for launch in the near future. A scientific estimate of the cost to properly dispose of all the chemical and metallic waste is ~9.5 million dollars.

The Pollution of Lake Okinawa
An Anthropogenic Lab

K.J. Sukhu

Quad Appeal

Official Statement:
"At this time our thoughts are with the families of those who are sick and dying. We also have members of our staff who have been affected by the illness. We want to assure the public that we have no liability and will launch our own investigation into the incident. Thank you."

Background Information:
Quad Appeal has a long running rivalry with its main competitor, Cross Switch. Both companies have been accused of exploiting child labor in the developing world in order to increase profits and stay competitive. To gain public support, Quad Appeal moved a few factories to North America. However, their expenses are closely monitored by the head office. It is reported that if their fiscal reports reflect a loss in even one quarter, these factories would be shut down despite having endured for quite some time.

Environmental Assessment:
This factory uses a large amount of leather, plastics, silicon, adhesives and chemical dyes. They employ roughly 4,000 workers and produce approximately 600,000 pairs of shoes and 200,000 hats each year. A scientific estimate of the cost to properly dispose of all the chemicals and waste is ~4.7 million dollars.

The Pollution of Lake Okinawa
An Anthropogenic Lab

K.J. Sukhu

Infinitysoft

Official Statement:
"At this time we will wait until the investigation is over before we release a statement from the company. We appreciate your patience and understanding. Thank you."

Background Information:
This is the first factory that Infinitysoft has opened in North America. All of its other factories are overseas. Infinitysoft has made billions of dollars in profit during the last few years and is one of the most lucrative electronics companies. Most of its profits are rumored to be the result of cheap labor. Infinitysoft pays their Seattle engineers well, but is alleged to pay their Asian workers who assemble their products next to nothing. Infinitysoft is fixated on increasing profits in any way they can. They have also filed several lawsuits against other companies such as Icon TC, Stasis Tech and Fickle (even though they themselves have been accused or ripping off an even larger company with a very similar product).

Environmental Assessment:
This company employs 2,000 workers. Amazingly they produce 100,000 Infinity-stars each month. A scientific estimate of the cost to properly dispose of all of the chemical and metallic waste is ~3.6 million dollars.

The Pollution of Lake Okinawa
An Anthropogenic Lab

K.J. Sukhu

Presidium Green

Official Statement:
"Presidium Green is devastated by this tragic event. We will fully co-operate with the police investigation until the truth is uncovered. Here at Presidium Green, we value our customers and strive to provide only the best products. Without our customers we are nothing and we hope that the public knows that we could not be responsible for this disaster."

Background Information:
Presidium Green has a reputation for manufacturing very well built products. However, they also have a history of not caring about their surroundings. Presidium Green was in a bit of controversy when it was rumored that many of its "Presidium Command 5" devices were being made from parts mined in African warzones. It was alleged that African warlords sold the company natural resources and used that money to buy weapons in order to intensify the fighting in those areas. Presidium has since been cleared of any wrong doing after a very short investigation yielded no concrete evidence. Presidium Green has also lost millions of dollars in the last few years. At the last shareholders meeting, the head office alluded to a company-wide restructuring plan.

Environmental Assessment:
This plant employs 2,500 workers. They are producing high resolution TVs which are capable of showing movies at a 4,000 resolution instead of 1080p. They produce 4,000 televisions each month and 30,000 Green-river players each week. A scientific estimate of the cost to properly dispose of all of the chemicals and metallic waste is ~4.3 million dollars.

The Pollution of Lake Okinawa
An Anthropogenic Lab

K.J. Sukhu

Stasis Tech

Official Statement:
"We at Stasis Tech feel deeply for the residents who have lost a loved one or have become sick. We are part of this community and are all weakened by a tragedy such as this. We hope that everyone recovers fully. We have provided a grief counselor for our workers and offer the same for any members of the community. When the town is strengthened, we're strengthened."

Background Information:
Stasis Tech is one of the world's most recognized electronics manufacturers. They create many of the components and pieces used in Infinitysoft and Fickle devices. However, they were recently taken to court over an Infinitysoft patent infringement law suit. They lost the lawsuit in North America but won their lawsuit in South Korea and Japan. It is believed that the company is annoyed with the American legal system. They are currently producing their new Solaris M9 smart phones. These phones could possibly be pulled from sale within the U.S. (due to the lawsuit) and so the plant has been under pressure to release them to the market as soon as possible.

Environmental Assessment:
This plant employs 2,900 workers. Amazingly they're able to produce 89,000 phones each month. A scientific estimate of the cost to properly dispose of all the chemical and metallic waste is ~6 million dollars

The Pollution of Lake Okinawa
An Anthropogenic Lab

K.J. Sukhu

Geographical Landscape

At the very North-East of the map lies the industrial complex. Furthest East is the Stasis Tech factory. Next to it (on the West side) is the Presidium Green factory. There is a large pond between the two factories which they share. Next to the Presidium Green factory (on the West side) is the Quad Appeal factory. There is a large river that runs through the property of the Quad Appeal factory which empties directly into Lake Okinawa. Next to the Quad Appeal factory is the Infinitysoft factory which has a pond directly North of it. Next to the Infinitysoft factory is the Xenoware Inc. factory. There is a large pond sitting next to the Xenoware Inc. factory as well.

In the middle of the map is Lake Okinawa. Directly West of the lake is a well that supplies the town of Jiftar and Soel. Jiftar is North-West of the lake and Soel is South-West of the lake. Directly East of the lake is the town of Erista. South of Erista is another well that is used as a secondary water source for the town. The main well of Erista is directly North of the town and is attached to the river that links the Quad Appeal factory to the lake. Directly South of Lake Okinawa is a large pond that is used as a water reserve for Soel. Directly North of the lake is a graveyard which is set to be turned into a site for oil drilling.

The Pollution of Lake Okinawa
An Anthropogenic Lab

K.J. Sukhu

Other Various Reports Gathered
Some may be true and some may be false

Mayor Jackson Mayor Jackson reported to local police that there was a "strange smell" coming from a few of the plants that have ponds next to them. However, she also stated that there was definitely a weird haze coming from the Quad Appeal factory a month ago.

Disgruntled Stasis Tech Employee An employee who was fired from Stasis Tech four days before the first reported illness, claims that managers would hold secret meetings after hours when employees went home. The angry employee says that they might have been illegally dumping something.

News Reporter James Wood works for a local paper. He claims that Presidium Green's plant manager has been under intense pressure to increase profits and cut costs.

International News A report states that Infinitysoft was getting ready to close the plant within a year, citing high costs for wages. The plant was given twelve months to increase the viability of its production or face closure.

Local Scientists The week of rain that the region received caused massive flooding in unusual places but was given little attention.

Erista City Council The week of intense heat resulted in the need to use some of the water from their secondary site for a few days. They also reported that Soel did the same thing.

Oil Company CEO The manager of Connected Petroleum has stated that the graveyard was to be dug up in a few months and oil drilling was set to begin. The company conducted some initial drilling tests, but no major operation had begun.

Environmental Group An environmental group says that for weeks Quad Appeal would not disclose their methods for chemical storage and disposal.

The Pollution of Lake Okinawa
An Anthropogenic Lab

K.J. Sukhu

Crazy Old Man Who Lives Close to the Factories	A man who is known to tell strange stories says that he saw men in Xenoware Inc. uniforms dumping things into the pond beside their factory.
Manager of Operations for Presidium Green, Stasis Tech & Infinitysoft	These companies have yet to allow an outside investigation of the ponds near their factories. However, Presidium Green says that it no longer has jurisdiction over the pond.
Xenoware Inc. Environmental Chief	"Xenoware filed our report on the cleanliness of the pond to the city weeks ago." Although this statement was confirmed by the mayor, the report seems to have vanished as no one can find it.
Financial Records of Soel	It seems that Xenoware and Presidium Green were paying higher taxes than the other companies.
Political Campaign Organizer	It seems that all the companies except for Presidium Green contributed to the campaign of the Mayor.
City Hall Office of Records	The majority of workers from Stasis Tech live in Erista. The majority of workers from Presidium Green live in either Erista or Jiftar. The majority of workers from Quad Appeal live in Soel. The majority of workers from Infinitysoft live in Jiftar. The majority of Xenoware Inc. employees come from Erista and Soel.
Well Known Plumber	Scott Odle, a popular plumber, said that the well between Jiftar and Soel received its water from Lake Okinawa and that the Town of Erista's secondary well gets its water from the lake as well. He speculates that the river from the Quad Appeal factory must be where the pollution enters the lake.
Geographical Surveyor	Due to recent flooding, a small stream has been created connecting Lake Okinawa and Soel's secondary pond.

The Pollution of Lake Okinawa
An Anthropogenic Lab

K.J. Sukhu

Really Old Citizen	The region's oldest citizen says that factories are one of the worst things to happen to the people of New Londo. He says Quad Appeal was the first to move in to the area and that Infinitysoft was the most recent factory to move in.
Avid Gardener	Jenny Nguyen is an avid gardener from the town of Erista. She claims that she used to have a large (illegal) garden South of Erista. However, a few weeks ago when she went to check on it, all the plants and flowers had died abruptly.
Duck Hunter Society	Jesse McNalley stated that the number of ducks in the area had recently decreased. He says that while Xenoware still has one or two birds on their properties it would be difficult to find any birds on Presidium Green, Stasis Tech or Infinitysoft grounds.
Urban Development Project	Gurpreet is an urban developer. He claims that he was to begin construction of a new town that was East of Soel. However, construction could not begin due to flooding and poor soil quality.
City Morgue	Many of the dead have been buried in a new gravesite South-West of the Lake.
Topography Expert	A topographic expert was quoted as saying, "This whole region is kind of strange in that the North is more elevated than the South but wind speeds, which come in from the North, typically remain high for this topography."
City Planner	Contracts and building permits for what was to be a new town South-West of the lake were abruptly cancelled, reworked and awarded to an electronics company that makes very small electronic components. The big recipient of the new contracts was James Anderson.
Presidium Green Spokesperson (Several Months Ago)	Presidium Green was reportedly making plans to lay off 400 workers. This idea was scrapped when a deal with Stasis Tech was reached. Stasis Tech paid Presidium Green an undisclosed amount of money to purchase some of their shared land.

The Pollution of Lake Okinawa
An Anthropogenic Lab

K.J. Sukhu

James Anderson	James is the brother of Geoffery Anderson who is the North American Regional Director of Presidium Green. He is on the record of being in favor of relocating the factory and has been quite outspoken on the topic.
Infinitysoft Lawyer	Stasis Tech's newest smartphone may be blocked from U.S. markets pending an appeal process. Stasis is therefore under pressure to increase revenues or cut costs before this is taken to court.
Independent Scientific Survey Team	After a thorough investigation, no barrels were found in Lake Okinawa. The report states that absolutely no illegal dumping occurred in Lake Okinawa. They did confirm, however, that the lake was mildly polluted.
Lobbyist	A lobbyist for Presidium Green was trying very hard to get the rules of where factories can be constructed changed. The bill almost passed but was rumored to have been stopped by lobbyists representing Xenoware Inc. and Stasis Tech.
Activist	Joe Linkin is known as somewhat of a criminal in New Londo. He has been jailed several times for theft, breaking and entering and trespassing. He calls himself a "political hero". He claims that one week ago he broke onto the grounds of Infinitysoft at night and took a sample of water from the river. He said that he slipped and fell in and lost the sample. Claiming the water was disgusting and full of chemicals, he also reported that he was feeling under the weather the next day but recovered soon thereafter.
Reports of CEO's	Each company claims that if the investigation points to them, they will do the following:

Xenoware Inc.:	"We will close up immediately and move the factory."
Infinitysoft:	"No decision has been made at this time."
Presidium Green:	"We will evaluate what the best outcome will be for our company and the town."
Quad Appeal:	"We will continue to work with this town and we will restructure."

The Pollution of Lake Okinawa
An Anthropogenic Lab

K.J. Sukhu

        Stasis Tech: "Similar to Xenoware we would close our factory and leave."

That is all the available data. There are many pieces of data that might be missing, but no one ever gets all the data. Using your scientific deductive strategies please try and solve the puzzle.

*Hint: Don't overlook the scientific data. Remember, you are a scientist solving a police case, not a police officer.

The Pollution of Lake Okinawa
An Anthropogenic Lab

K.J. Sukhu

What Should I Hand In?

1. A Detailed Map of New Londo

You will hand in a detailed map of New Londo. The map should include as many features such as lakes, factories, wells, etc.

> Hint: Make sure this map is as correct and complete as possible. It will not only help you solve the case but it will help to enhance the evidence that you will present.

2. Company Evidence

You will fill the Company Profile sheets. You will state the guilt or innocence of the company and explain your reasoning for either their guilt or innocence. You will also need to create an original logo for each company.

The Pollution of Lake Okinawa
An Anthropogenic Lab

K.J. Sukhu

The Map of New Londo

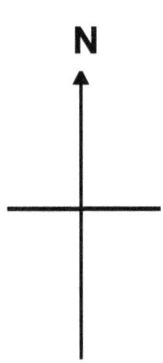

The Pollution of Lake Okinawa
An Anthropogenic Lab

K.J. Sukhu

Company Profile

Company: _____

[Company Logo]

GUILTY or **INNOCENT**

(circle one)

Reasoning/Evidence

_____
_____
_____
_____
_____
_____
_____
_____
_____
_____
_____
_____
_____
_____
_____
_____
_____
_____
_____

The Pollution of Lake Okinawa
An Anthropogenic Lab

K.J. Sukhu

Company Profile

Company: _____

Company Logo

GUILTY   or   INNOCENT

(circle one)

Reasoning/Evidence

_____
_____
_____
_____
_____
_____
_____
_____
_____
_____
_____
_____
_____
_____
_____
_____
_____
_____
_____

The Pollution of Lake Okinawa
An Anthropogenic Lab

K.J. Sukhu

Company Profile

Company: _____

[Company Logo]

GUILTY   or   INNOCENT

(circle one)

Reasoning/Evidence

_____
_____
_____
_____
_____
_____
_____
_____
_____
_____
_____
_____
_____
_____
_____
_____
_____
_____
_____

The Pollution of Lake Okinawa
An Anthropogenic Lab

K.J. Sukhu

Company Profile

Company: _____

[Company Logo]

GUILTY   or   INNOCENT

(circle one)

Reasoning/Evidence

_____
_____
_____
_____
_____
_____
_____
_____
_____
_____
_____
_____
_____
_____
_____
_____
_____
_____

The Pollution of Lake Okinawa   K.J. Sukhu
An Anthropogenic Lab

Company Profile

Company: _____

Company Logo

GUILTY   or   INNOCENT

(circle one)

Reasoning/Evidence

_____
_____
_____
_____
_____
_____
_____
_____
_____
_____
_____
_____
_____
_____
_____
_____
_____
_____
_____
_____

The Mysterious Seven of Drewersville

An investigation using DNA, blood samples, and
reports to solve a series of murders

The Mysterious Seven of Drewersville K.J. Sukhu
A Crime Scene Inquiry Lab

Background

A small town not known for violence has recently uncovered several troubling cases. Foul play has been suspected in each incident. Dead bodies have been found either burned or mutilated beyond recognition, people are missing from the town, two people are thought to have been kidnapped and one is badly burned and lies in a coma. The deaths appear to be relatively recent. Most residents are scared and dumbfounded. In the town's 86 year history they have only experienced minor graffiti problems and domestic violence reports, but nothing of this magnitude. The local police were not equipped to handle such a delicate investigation, so other agencies were brought in to solve the mystery. However, several levels of law enforcement claimed jurisdiction and so the investigation has stalled. In fact, the situation is turning into a political quagmire. So, in a last ditch effort to solve the case, the investigators have decided to turn to a team of scientists to investigate the situation.

A public inquiry will soon take place to see why this investigation has dragged on for so long. Therefore, you don't have much time to solve the case. You must find out **how the individuals died, who was possibly kidnapped**, the **identity of the murderer(s)** and the **motives behind it all**.

To make matters worse, you can't actually enter the town because it has been quarantined. So, not only are you going to have to figure out this case, you're going to have to do it from a secondary location.

To Help You Solve the Case You Will Have the Following Information

1. **Suspect Background Information**
   - The police did a great job narrowing down the possible suspects.
2. **An Incomplete List of Victims**
   - You will have to change and update this list as you go through the evidence.
3. **Suspect Interviews Taken by Various Police Departments**
   - These statements aren't complete, but at least there's something right?!?
4. **Geographical Landscape**
   - Figuring out the layout of Drewersville and the proximity of people to locations may help your investigation.
5. **List of Missing People**
   - With many people missing in the town, it stands to reason that some of the missing may be victims.

6. Reports Gathered from Various Police Agencies
- Even the smallest detail may be worth checking out.

7. Listening Devices Planted
- The police planted several "bugs" around town. You can use this information to help your case, but you shouldn't soley rely on it.

8. Blood Analysis
- Looking at someone's blood samples might seem useless, but in some investigations it might be fruitful.

9. DNA Analysis
- The DNA will help to narrow down victims and culprits, but DNA alone is not enough to convict. A motive and logical story must compliment the DNA.

10. Objects of Significance Found
- DNA found on dead bodies, letters and materials near the victims. This is sure to be helpful.

The Mysterious Seven of Drewersville
A Crime Scene Inquiry Lab

K.J. Sukhu

Suspect Background Information
A list of suspects thought to have committed the crimes

To get you started, information from the previous investigators have been reviewed/provided and, although they can't agree on who's in charge, they pretty much have all agreed on who their main suspects are.

Suspect 1
Mervin Padolski (Age: 23)

Mervin is a rather conflicting character. He tends to keep to himself, but is also known to be quite an eccentric young man. Throughout his high school years he was a loner. He often clashed with many students. He seemed to take pleasure in playing "devil's advocate". He was suspended several times for "inciting problems at school" but nothing major. He left Drewersville for college, and vowed never to return. However, two years into his four year program, he suddenly returned. No one is really sure why he did but he has become even more of a nuisance than before he left. The police have a growing file on his misdemeanors which include unlawful protest, disturbing the peace and illegally dumping garbage.

Suspect 2
Sherwin Makazaki (Age: 36)

Sherwin is the offspring of an interracial marriage. His father was stationed in Japan over forty years ago. Sherwin grew up on the island resort of Okinawa and became a fisherman. He was quite successful and lived a comfortable life. However, commercial fishing crippled his once thriving business and forced him to go further offshore to make a living. This practice however, couldn't sustain itself as the fishing region was being contested by China, Japan and the United States (with all three sending out ships to discourage fishing). Unfortunately, Sherwin had to sell his business and decided to look for work. He found employment in Drewersville, where he now works for a local fishery. It's been a difficult transition having been previously self employed to now being accountable to other people.

Suspect 3
Frank Duchovney (Age: 37)

Frank is the owner of "Duchovney Tuna". He inherited the business from his father, Giuseppe. Giuseppe, came to Drewersville with nothing and built a thriving business that sells packaged tuna all over the world. At its peak the factory employed 50% of the residents of Drewersville. Today, due to automated machines, the total amount of residents employed is roughly 5%. Giuseppe recently passed away of natural causes. However, Frank is very bitter over his father's death and resents many people in the town. He felt that his father wasn't treated well by local doctors during his battle with cancer. In addition, a political decision based on a re-zoning issue which makes way for a new condo development has forced Frank to move his factory. It also seems that this decision was supported by the people in an effort to increase tourism and decrease taxes. Frank has resented the townspeople ever since. If it were not for his dad's factory, the town would not be what it is today.

Suspect 4
Adol Vice (Age: 41)

Adol is an Austrian monk with a thick accent. He recently moved to the town to work at the church as part of a missionary exchange. He's had a hard time fitting in with the locals. Many describe him as a very private person. He has been in a few altercations with church staff over protocols and tradition. He believes that the church and the townspeople are not living right in the eyes of the Creator. In fact, he has dedicated several sermons to reasons why people are heading for damnation. Due to these extremist views, attendance by his congregation has dropped sharply, causing prominent members in charge of the missionary exchange to reassess him as a candidate. They have threatened to review his role in the church if he doesn't increase membership. This has caused Adol to become extremely disillusioned with church leaders.

Suspect 5
Jason Barret (Age: 51)

Jason is a prominent politician. He started out as a school principal and served the community for fifteen years before becoming the deputy mayor. Eventually he became the mayor for a brief stint at which time he ran for the senate and won. Although he travels to the capital, he is based out of Drewersville. Usually outspoken, he has become withdrawn from the public eye. He recently started cancelling all of his public engagements. He has also fired a few members of his office staff and hired members who would normally be considered underqualified. Recently he has been spending more time away from Drewersville. Additionally, a newly leaked document disclosed that his votes in the capital have been marked by "no-shows".

Suspect 6
Sidney Vatz (Age: 29)

Sidney is widely known around town for his wild, decadent ways. He is the son of a fisherman, but if you were to look at him he could easily pass as the son of a wealthy man. He is known for buying expensive things which the average Drewersville citizen could not afford. He recently opened up a gentleman's club (which the town greatly opposed). No one knows where or how he earns his money. He is a highly secretive and suspicious character.

The Mysterious Seven of Drewersville
A Crime Scene Inquiry Lab

K.J. Sukhu

Suspect 7
Jacob Franc (Age: 35) – DECEASED

Jacob was a young business type. Determined to make a name for himself, he made it clear that he wanted to start a business. He soon went to work for Frank. He learned the business quickly and helped improve the company's finances. However, he wasn't seeing any bonuses. Frank felt that giving "this kid" the experience was a bonus in itself but Jacob wanted more. Jacob decided to take a second look into Frank's business and ended up discovering some significant inefficiencies that could be improved upon. Instead of informing Frank, he decided to quietly look into opening up a competing business. When Frank discovered this, a physical altercation broke out. That wouldn't be the last physical altercation the two would have though.

In an apparent murder-suicide, a note written by Jacob was recovered at his condo near the docks. The note outlined where authorities could find his body as well as that of his victim, Jeremy Toure. Authorities found both bodies burned and one with a bullet wound to the cranium of Jacob. It's suspected that after Jacob burned Jeremy, he shot himself and his limp body fell into the fire as well.

The Mysterious Seven of Drewersville
A Crime Scene Inquiry Lab

K.J. Sukhu

An Incomplete List of Victims
Here is an incomplete list of the data obtained thus far

The information is scant. It's your job to figure out their identities as well as find out who killed them and why. Remember, even if you link them with evidence, you must provide a motive.

Victim 1
Description: A burned body was found in a small ditch in the forest behind the town's baseball stadium.
Gender: Unknown
Identity: Unknown

Victim 2
Description: A victim was found dead and placed in an open grave in the graveyard. His body was partially burned.
Gender: Male
Identity: The body is presumed to be that of Jeremy Toure (suspected victim of a murder-suicide)

Description: Although not classified as a victim, a body was severely burned and suffered what is thought to be a self-inflicted gunshot wound.
Gender: Male
Identity: Jacob Franc

Victim 3
Description: A body was found burned and dumped in the bottom of the lake in the park.
Gender: Female
Identity: Unknown

Victim 4
Description: Possibly kidnapped.
Gender: Unknown
Identity: Unknown

Victim 5
Description: Possibly kidnapped.
Gender: Unknown
Identity: Unknown

Victim 6
Description: Suffered severe burning and is currently in a coma.
Gender: Female
Identity: Stacy McEnroe

Victim 7
Description: A partially burned body was dumped and left underneath the docks.
Gender: Unknown
Identity: Unknown

The Mysterious Seven of Drewersville   K.J. Sukhu
A Crime Scene Inquiry Lab

Suspect Interviews Taken by Various Police Departments

Official statements taken from suspects

Unfortunately the suspects were not interrogated by the same department. Instead, interrogators from various agencies were involved and each used different techniques.

Excerpt from statement compiled by SMPD for Mervin Padolski:
"I couldn't murder anyone [even toned]. I'm not that type of person. I'll level with you. I hate the residents of this town. They're idiots. They're a bunch of hillbillies that only care about their idiotic, useless problems [voice rising]. They need to grow up and [pause]… sorry I haven't been feeling well lately [pause]. I'm sick [pause]. If you guys could go into my place you could pick up my medicine and search my apartment. I've got nothing to hide… really. But I'm tired and I need my medicine. I can barely function without my medicine."

Excerpt from statement compiled by RCPD for Sherwin Makazaki:
"I loved her, but I hated what she did [frustrated]. When I met her I never knew what she did. I wouldn't have gone out with her if I did [regret]. She ruined my honour. I told my family about her [pause]. They still ask me how she's doing. I had to lie to them and tell them she's fine [grief]. I can't tell them about the situation, I've already failed enough in my life [anger/grief]. I loved her [pause] I love her [pause] I didn't kill her [yelling]! That's why I'm here, right? You think I killed her because she's missing? I could never hurt her [yelling]! This situation is so…"

Excerpt from statement compiled by RCPD for Frank Duchovney:
"I don't know why I'm here. Honestly, this is ridiculous [even toned]. I'm not answering anything until my lawyer is contacted. You know, I can't believe I'm even here [annoyed]. You shouldn't be looking at me. You should be talking to those criminal politicians, Kadri and Gomez. They're the real criminals. They just accused me because they want to drag my family's name through the mud [anger]. When things change and the town is in hard times and everyone turns to my company to save them once again, I'll remember this [pleasure]."

Excerpt from statement compiled by TMPD for Adol Vice:
"[laughing] You boys better tread carefully. I serve a higher power. I don't answer to the likes of you. If you repent and confess your sins to me then you may save yourself from the corruption that is swallowing this town. I asked for righteous justice and guess what? [pleasure] This town has prostitutes, drug dealers, even the common man has dirty secrets. I say this whole place can go to…"

The Mysterious Seven of Drewersville
A Crime Scene Inquiry Lab

K.J. Sukhu

Excerpt from interview compiled by SMPD for Jason Barret

Lawyer: "You don't have to make a statement."

Mr. Barret: "It's ok. I have nothing to hide [even tone]."

Interrogator: "Can you explain where you were and who you were with on Thursday, February 12th, at 7:30pm, Mr. Barret?"

Mr. Barret: "I… I don't recall who I was with or what I was doing."

The interrogator shows Mr. Barret a picture.

Mr. Barret looks at his lawyer.

Lawyer: "My client will not answer any more questions at this time. Thank you."

Excerpt from interview compiled by SMPD for Sidney Vatz:

Interviewer: "So, Sidney you lead a pretty lavish lifestyle, huh?"

Sidney: "I do alright [annoyed]."

Interviewer: "Comfy in your new condo?"

Sidney: "It's ok, but I'm looking for something bigger [mocking]."

Interviewer: "How's business? Can't imagine it's going well, considering the backlash you've received opening it up."

Sidney: [smirk] "Like I said, I do alright. You'd be surprised at the people who publicly hate it and secretly love it. Maybe you should come by. I'll buy you a drink [mocking]."

Interviewer: "My records indicate that you've been on welfare for the last few years… is that correct?"

Sidney: [silence]

Interviewer: "Where did you get the money to open up your club?"

Sidney: "I want my lawyer."

The Mysterious Seven of Drewersville
A Crime Scene Inquiry Lab

K.J. Sukhu

Geographical Landscape
A description of Drewersville

Having a visual map of Drewersville may or may not aid you in this case.

At the very North-Western corner of the map, there is a large sign that says "Welcome to Drewersville: The Land of Rain". South of the sign, Route 77, you will find the church. Behind the church is the graveyard. Across the street (Eastward) is the baseball diamond. North-East of the diamond is a forest. Directly East of the diamond is the general store. East of the general store is the Veterans' Club where the veterans congregate. Next to the veterans' lodge is a library and next to that is the post office. Across Liberty Street are two small assembly factories. In the centre of Drewersville one can find City Hall. The building is a curved three part structure which wraps around a large statue of Prometheus. The statue holds the world in one hand and fire in the other. From the church if you continue South, down Route 77 past Liberty Street, you will pass a medium sized pond connected to a well on the West side. A little further South on the East side you will find the tuna factory. Continue South, down Route 77 and it will eventually curve East. On the bottom left of the map you will find the docks. Near the docks is a fishing restaurant and South-East you will find a beach and boardwalk. Near this location you will find the new condo development that boasts three new buildings. South-East of City Hall you will find a large park that is protected under the environmental act.

The Mysterious Seven of Drewersville
A Crime Scene Inquiry Lab

K.J. Sukhu

List of Missing People
A list of possible victims

While it remains unclear exactly who the victims are, it is widely known across this small town those who have abruptly vanished.

Dr. Allen:
Dr. Allen has been serving the people of Drewersville for some time. His practice is highly successful and he enjoys the private life offered in a smaller town. Serving a smaller community offers him a higher salary and more time to himself. If he's not at his practice, he's usually on vacation. The doctor is addicted to traveling and is usually gone for weeks at a time. Since these incidents have started however, no one has been able to contact him.

Alfred Gomez:
Alfred Gomez is a convicted child predator. At the age of 20 he went out with a girl who was 16. When her parents found out about the relationship, they called the police and after an extensive investigation, it was found that the two had engaged in inappropriate behavior. As a result Alfred was convicted of statutory rape and sentenced to 5 years in jail. Since he's been out, the townspeople have treated him very poorly. He cannot get a job because of his criminal record and he can't continue with his schooling. Many people hate Alfred, and it seems to be acceptable to voice their disgust. Alfred has been missing for the past few weeks. There is a possibility that he may have left town for a fresh start.

Amy Droden:
Amy is a very quiet girl. Many people would categorize her as somewhat of a loner and she has been the subject of many rumors throughout town. At the age of 16 she had an inappropriate relationship with an older man. When her parents found out, the relationship ended abruptly. Since then it's been hard for her to make friends or really socialize with anyone. The few relationships she once had fizzled out long ago. She tried to leave the town when she turned 19 but couldn't afford to. She has been working at the local convenience store, attempting to save money for the past two years. She has since vanished. She did not tell anyone where she was going so this is very suspicious behavior.

Anthony Plexi:
Anthony Plexi, is the owner and operator of "PlexiFish". Anthony employs most of the fisherman of Drewersville and is the major supplier of tuna to "Duchovney Tuna". He is a pleasant man, whom the majority respect. He is entering his twilight years but still works as hard as ever.

The Mysterious Seven of Drewersville
A Crime Scene Inquiry Lab

K.J. Sukhu

Brady Spark:
Brady is a retired veteran. Ever since the war he's come back changed. He's been quiet and alone in his thoughts. He slowly neglected his loved ones and they've drifted apart emotionally. He's older now and his only friend, his thoughts, are starting to betray him. He's been diagnosed with Alzheimer's. With no family to care for him, he relies on the group at the Veterans' Club. Lately, however, the group has been preoccupied. One day they just realized how preoccupied they were. Spark is gone and no one knows where he might be.

Danny Arc:
Danny is a kept man. He's never had a job. Instead, he finds an older woman, romances her, feeds off her money, and when there is nothing left, moves on to the next one. He's cocky, flamboyant, athletic, good looking and a failed actor, who believes the world owes him something. He came to Drewersville a few years ago. He's angered more than a few people since he's been there. It wouldn't be a surprise if he skipped town or he ended up in one of the body bags.

Duncan Mancini:
Duncan works at the post office. He very much enjoys the ease of sorting and delivering mail. It offers him a steady pay rate and time to work on his hobby. He is an amateur computer software programmer. He was developing an "app" that used a "GPS" that would allow him to track packages in real time. Things were going smoothly as the "app" had several successful test trials. However, after a while, he found himself using the app for different purposes. It seemed that he had a second hobby, stalking people. It was discovered when a co-worker found his "log" book. After the co-worker questioned him, he bolted. No one has seen him since.

Jake Slow:
Jake was the minister of Drewersville before the missionary exchange with Adol Vice. He has been described as a mild mannered man who really loved the town and its citizens. When he was offered the chance to preach in Austria, he was very hesitant. It was only to be for two years but Jake was happy where he was. With the prospect of ministering to more people and spreading the word, he decided to go for it. However, a year into the exchange with Adol Vice, he developed cold feet and wanted to return home. The committee who set up the exchange did not want the program to fail so they pressured Jake to stay. They gave him an ultimatum; finish his time in Austria or be removed from his ministry altogether. Angered by the ultimatum, Jake quit, citing that he would return home and continue with his congregation whether the committee liked it or not. Records indicate that he was on a plane that flew home, but no one has any idea of what happened to him since.

The Mysterious Seven of Drewersville
A Crime Scene Inquiry Lab

K.J. Sukhu

Mohamed Aljeer:
Mohamed came into town about a year ago and opened a Pakistani restaurant. The food was delicious but the town never gave it a chance. Instead people complained of the smell, and were very rude to him. Determined not to let his business fail, he included local food on the menu to attract more customers. He even hired local students to help bring a friendly atmosphere to the restaurant. For a time it worked. The real problem came when one day, a patron came in and saw one of his hired students passively flipping through his religious material. The patron spread the word that Mohamed was indoctrinating the town's kids. The town protested the restaurant until one night it was closed and Mohamed was gone.

Stacy Florense:
Stacy is a waitress who works at Vatz's Gentleman's Club. She's not the warmest girl. She hates the job and can't stand the guys who frequent the club. She feels sick having to make small talk with them. She's been caught spitting in patrons' food before serving it and has been warned. Disgusted with people, she approached Duncan to help her design a website. The website was supposed to "out" the men who visited Vatz's Gentleman's Club. She never got the website going however, because Duncun left before he could finish coding it. She approached a few other people before reaching a dead end. The next thing you know, she too disappeared.

Stacy McEnroe:
Stacy is a young lady who just finished her undergraduate degree. She decided she was going to take a few years off before persuing a law degree. She got a job as an office secretary at City Hall. However, she was disillusioned with her position. She felt that she shouldn't be the one taking messages but rather, that people should be taking hers. She started to make decisions that weren't approved, and eventually she got fired. She was mortified and appalled that people she thought were below her had the authority to fire her. She hadn't been seen for a while until she mysteriously showed up in the hospital in dire condition. Burns to her body were significant. Doctors decided to induce a coma in order to give her a fighting chance.

Jeremy Toure: DECEASED
Jeremy was the soon-to-be business partner of Jacob Franc. The two were set to open their own fish processing plant. However, before they could open, they were sued by "Duchovney Tuna". Before they went to court however, it seems that Frank had a change of heart and only sued Jacob, leaving Toure out of the court proceedings. It's unknown as to why Jeremy was dropped from the lawsuit.

IMPORTANT: This report contains proprietary and original material. Accordingly, this document may not be copied or released to third parties without consent.

The Mysterious Seven of Drewersville
A Crime Scene Inquiry Lab

K.J. Sukhu

Reports Gathered from Various Police Agencies
Some reports may be true and some may be false…beware

The police agencies did a great job of taking statements from various people. It's now up to you to put all the pieces together.

Official Press Release from Mayor Bishop's Office	"We at City Hall hope that our friend, Mr. Barret, is proven innocent as quickly as possible. We would like to have the guilty parties arrested and put this unpleasant business behind us. We need to stop focusing on the negative and get back to what makes this town great."
News Journalist	"Apparently Barret canned his personal aide, Janson, in an unprecedented move. The move seemed strange seeing that Barret just recently proclaimed that if anyone was to continue his legacy, it would most likely be Janson. Janson could not be reached for comment."
News Reporter	"This year the senate race is going to be very tight. Kadri and Barret are neck and neck, in the opinion polls. To be honest, I'm kinda surprised that Barret hasn't pulled out of the senate race."
Choir Leader	"Listen, most people in town can't stand Vice, but there are a lot of people who have started to take what he says very seriously. The ones that do still attend church and are very loyal to the guy."
Bank Manager	"Vatz did come in to look into a loan for his gentleman's club but there was no way he could get approved for that. First, he had no job, and second, this town never wanted his club to begin with. I'm not sure where he got the money, to be honest."
Local Resident	"I wish I never voted for Barret. It makes me sick he's suspected of this. Next time I'll vote for two good politicians, like Kadri and Gomez."

The Mysterious Seven of Drewersville K.J. Sukhu
A Crime Scene Inquiry Lab

Veterans' Club	"The people they got running this place are completely removed from what's important. The only man in town who actually makes sense is Adol Vice. People don't like him because he's aggressive, but at least he has some moral fiber."
Condo Development Manager	"This has been a really great project to work on. Myself and the architect have had no problems at all. The only thing that's come from City Hall is these dang statues that they want us to build. Their measurements are so specific and it seems so unnecessary."
Local Resident	"That politician Kadri is kind of slimy. He only recently started attending church. I'm guessing he's trying to gain political favor with citizens by attending."
Drewersville Tourism Shop	"Drewersville has so many attractions. We have a beach, a protected forest, which, might I say, is one of the only places that boasts a beautiful lake that has bass, king mackerel and pike."
Nurse Claire	"I can confirm that Mervin is being treated for a virus similar to the Rhizidiovirus. Currently he is taking a few NRTI's prescribed by Dr. Allen. Unfortunately, I cannot tell you more than that due to patient doctor confidentiality. I'm trying to contact the doctor but he hasn't returned any calls since he went on vacation."
Local Gardener	"Business has picked up recently. Two up and coming local politicians just gave me a contract to plant this neat white flower around several sites. The flower's white and has a yellow centre. I forget the name of it, but I think that they import it from the Swiss."
Old Police File	Makazaki was investigated in a previous case. He was dating the accountant who was charged with defrauding Anthony Plexi's fishing company. Sherwin was later cleared as it turned out that the relationship had ended abruptly when news came out that Makazaki had cheated on her.

The Mysterious Seven of Drewersville
A Crime Scene Inquiry Lab

K.J. Sukhu

Police Surveillance	During the time Vatz was held, there was a spike in the number of people who visited the back of the gentleman's club. They go there and just wait for extended periods of time and then just leave.
Store Clerk	"Arc used to come in everyday and buy a lotto ticket, protein shake and milk. Strange guy. That's about all I can tell you."
Local Fisherman	"Makazaki and Tony? They're both the same. They got the same work ethic and the same stubborn attitude. If it's a good day and you're out with the two of them, then you're busting your hump non-stop for 12 hours. If it's a bad day, then you get to hear them arguing with one another for 12 hours. Those two got their own issues."
Former Investigator	"Three letters were sent to us… they were strange. One of them seemed a little different than the other two."
Local Resident	"I hate Frank. At first I felt bad for the guy, having to move his factory, but the relocation was covered by tax payers. He also got to choose from several sites where to relocate his factory. He ended up moving closer to the residential community at Liberty and 77. Now the place smells like tuna. I think he did it to piss everyone off."
Old Lady	"Duncan's a creepy fellow. Who designs a tool so they can stalk someone? To think he was the one to process the town's mail…. hmmph. What other applications did he invent?"
Choir Boy	"I wish Minister Slow would come back. Until he does, we're stuck with Adol Vice… but what do I know? I'm just a choir boy… a choir boy."
Newspaper Editor	"A total of three letters were sent to the police. Each is as creepy as the next. Who could do such a thing? Makes for a great story though. Whoever wanted the attention sure is getting it."

The Mysterious Seven of Drewersville
A Crime Scene Inquiry Lab

K.J. Sukhu

Gentleman's Club Patron	"Yeah, Arc always came in here. He and Vatz were good buddies. At least I think they were. Anyhow when he came here he'd go straight to the back. Him and Vatz would talk for a bit and then he'd come out and hang out with us. Decent guy, I guess, but a bit of a loud mouth. He would always tell us about all the wives he used to hook up with."
Stock Advisor	"It's tough to hear that Plexi's missing. I hope he's on vacation... although for him it seems out of character. He could use some time away. Things got messy when Frank tried to buy up most of the shares from "PlexiFish" after Anthony took the company public. It was crazy when Kadri stepped in and put a stop to it."
Therapist	"Yes, I've been treating both Sherwin and Mervin… interesting fellows. However, that's all I can say due to doctor patient confidentiality."
Construction Worker	"My contract has been put on hold until this mess is cleared up. I was supposed to take down the Duchovney mansion. He finally decided to move. I guess it must have been that electronics factory that just opened up. It's almost right next to the man's house."
Paparazzi	"It's difficult to get to the Senator's Mansion. It's on a hill way in the back of the forest. Add this to the fact that he never leaves his house, it's really difficult to get a picture."
Forest Ranger	"Padolski is harmless. The town just knows he's a little crazy, but physically he's weak. Even if he wanted to hurt someone I don't think he could. Anyhow, we've turned a blind eye to him living in a little shack in the park. That way he can't bother anyone in town, he's out of the way and we can monitor him."
Ex-Church Member	"I stopped going to church because of Adol. He's too extreme for me and the kids. But now my husband's just started going to church. He usually spent his time at the Veterans' Club but now when he's not there, he's at church. It's a touchy topic at home."

IMPORTANT: This report contains proprietary and original material. Accordingly, this document may not be copied or released to third parties without consent.

The Mysterious Seven of Drewersville
A Crime Scene Inquiry Lab

K.J. Sukhu

Town Gossip	"Ever see Sherwin in short sleeves? Of course you haven't. It's because he is severely depressed. He had an issue with um… cutting. Don't ask me how I know and you didn't hear that from me."
Condo Developer	"Yeah the new condos got snatched up pretty quickly. Everyone's buying them so they can rent them out to tourists. The bank must have been helpful in procuring loans because many of the locals were able to come up with the money easily."
Sandra Droden	"I'm worried sick about my little girl. Who knows where she could be? I know that pervert's got something to do with it. I'm so worried about her. I still remember the day that strange boy came and told me about my daughter and that perv. It makes me so angry! He ruined her life!"
Herbalist	"The best remedy is sometimes being in touch with oneself. I recommend to all my patients that they speak with a man of the cloth in order to help clear their mind and purify them."
Investor	"This isn't the country I grew up in. A man owns a tuna factory and then wants to own the vessels that transport the tuna to the factory and politicians call that a monopoly? What type of world is this?"
Internal Memo from the Desk of Gomez	As for the statues, the restoration of City Hall is also to boast a small improvement. The right hand shall face North-East 36° while the left hand will face North-West 48°. For the statues in the condo development; their right hand should also point in the same direction but the left hand should point North-West 16°. Any deviation and all public contracts will be lost.
Crazy Racist	"I told Stacy not to mix races. Now, I'm not a racist or anything, but I think that races shouldn't mix. We are a dying race and what that girl was doing was a disgrace. Of course she's missing if she got messed up with that boy. Look what happened to the kids who worked for that brown boy."

The Mysterious Seven of Drewersville
A Crime Scene Inquiry Lab

K.J. Sukhu

Internal Commission Board Spokesperson	"Barret's campaign is being investigated for accepting funds over the legal limit. It seems that a local businessman paid $10,000 during last year's campaign fund drive."
Bank Records	It seems that Nurse Claire was able to aggressively pay off her mortgage as she increased monthly payments by almost 74%.
Police Officer	"Actually, Spark is the reason we found the first body to begin with. We were looking all over for him. City Hall told us to spare no expense in our search for the guy. It seemed that that was our number one goal; to find him. City Hall gave us a crazy budget. We scoured the town and we couldn't find him. But we uncovered this crazy show."

Listening Devices Planted
The police have planted several "bugs" throughout Drewersville

The police planted several listening devices throughout Drewersville. Some yielded helpful info, some not as much. Hopefully it can help in the investigation.

Bugged Condo Apartment

Makazaki: "どうしたらいいか分からないよ。お母さん、あの人たちは僕が誰かを殺したって思ってるよ。"

????: [unintelligible garble]

Makazaki: "勿論そんなのしてないよ。"

????: [unintelligible garble]

Makazaki: "その女の子に出会って恋に落ちたんだけど、彼女はエキゾチックなダンサーだったんだ。"

????: [unintelligible garble]

Makazaki: "それが家族に恥をかかせることぐらい分かってるよ。"

????: [unintelligible garble]

Makazaki: "それでも、僕はしてないよ。"

????: [unintelligible garble]

Makazaki: "僕がバカだからライターオイルを買ったのは僕だと、きっとあの人たちは思うよ。クラブを燃やそうと思ったけど、でも出来なかったんだ。殺された人が燃やされてても、僕のアパートを捜索したら、きっとあの人たちは僕が犯人だと思うに決まってるよ。"

Bug Malfunction

* Note: The fragment translator is not entirely fluent, but it's just enough that it may be helpful.

The Mysterious Seven of Drewersville K.J. Sukhu
A Crime Scene Inquiry Lab

Senator's House

Barret:	"It's going to come out sooner or later."
????:	"How can you be sure? You were pretty good about keeping it a secret."
Barret:	"Why did this have to happen? Especially now. You know I won't survive against that slimeball Kadri right?"
????:	"Time will tell. Plus you have bigger problems."
Barret:	"Yeah, you're right. It doesn't help that I'm being investigated for the funds from Frank either, you know."
????:	"I know."
Barret:	"I should have just divorced my wife after last year's senate race."
????:	[silence]
Barret:	"You take care of that thing we needed?"
????:	"Yeah."
Barret:	"Good. At least that's one headache gone".
????:	[silence]
Barret:	"How's my girl doing anyways? I hope she's alright."
????:	"She's fine."
Barret:	"Good. Anyhow, this will all blow over and you will get everything that's coming to you. I promise."

Doctor's Office

Nurse Claire:	"It's been great working here. I do whatever I want and I've been getting great bonuses."
????:	"Why so good?"
Nurse Claire:	"I stumbled on this one day."

The Mysterious Seven of Drewersville   K.J. Sukhu
A Crime Scene Inquiry Lab

????: "What is it?"

Nurse Claire: "Just listen."

> Dr. Allen: "But I love you."
> ????: "Listen it may be ok for you but I can't afford for this to come out. I've worked too hard. Not now anyway."
> Dr. Allen: "I'm tired of all the secrecy, all the "vacations". I've given you everything you want. You want more? I can get you more, no problem, why can't we just…"

[click]

????: "Hey! Play more."

Nurse Claire: "No way … my little secret."

City Hall

Gomez: "I approved that factory next to Frank's house. Kadri didn't. If anyone is to blame for the mercury in the lake, it's not Kadri."

????: [unintelligible garble]

Gomez: "Wait, there must be a deal we can work out!"

????: [unintelligible garble]

Gomez: "I'll have to get it approved."

????: [unintelligible garble]

Gomez: "Let me talk to Kadri and the master… we'll see what we can do."

Church

"You're all teaching your children to worship the devil. You teach your children to welcome the devil into your house. Teach them to provide milk and cookies to the devil. Teach them that the devil will bring them presents if they obey him. Let me ask you disgusting sinners several questions. What being is omnipresent? Do you truants even know what omnipresent means? It means everywhere, all the time. Well, guess what? You teach your child that Santa Claus can travel around the globe in one night. Who is the only one who can judge you? You sheep teach your kids that Santa can judge them because he is making a list and checking it twice and he will deem who is naughty or nice. Rearrange the letters of Santa. What do you get? You get Satan. So go home and teach your children to worship Santa if you want to burn in….."

The Mysterious Seven of Drewersville
A Crime Scene Inquiry Lab

K.J. Sukhu

Veterans' Club

Adol Vice: "Es ist mir egal, was der Austausch sagt! Es ist klar, dass diese Stadt der Sünde gereinigt werden muss. Ich bin der einzige, der es tun kann."

????: [unintelligible garble]

Adol Vice: "Ich werde dieser Stadt ein Beispiel meiner Kräfte zeigen."

????: [unintelligible garble]

Adol Vice: " Wie eine große Flamme, werde ich das Böse ihrer Sünde reinigen und ein neues Zeitalter des Wohlstands herbeiführen."

????: [unintelligible garble]

Adol Vice: "Dann und nur dann werde ich nach Österreich zurück, um die Kirche zu führen. Alle Sünde muss verworfen/ ausgeschlossen werden und alle Sünder müssen Buße tun. Das ist meine Berufung!"

Bank

Bank Teller: "One second, I have to see if I can approve this."

Vatz: "What do you mean? This cheque is good."

Bank Teller: "Yes. But I can't approve a deposit of this size. I have to get the manager."

[inaudible whispering]

Bank Manager: "Hi. What can I do for you today?"

Vatz: "I'm trying to cash out this cheque."

Bank Manager: "May I see it please? How much do you want to cash out?"

Vatz: "All $8,000."

Bank Manager: "Unfortunately we're not equipped to allow a withdrawal of that size. You'll need to arrange it so that we can protect everyone's safety. However, we can deposit the cheque. [pause] I'm sorry, Mr. Vatz. Given that this cheque is from a missing person, we cannot deposit it."

The Mysterious Seven of Drewersville   K.J. Sukhu
A Crime Scene Inquiry Lab

Gentleman's Club

Vatz: "That'll be $2,500."

????: [unintelligible garble]

Vatz: "The price is $1,600."

????: [unintelligible garble]

Vatz: "No, that's not worth my time."

????: [unintelligible garble]

Vatz: "I don't care where or how you get the money. But the price is non-negotiable. You're welcome to go find another distributor but we both know I'm the only game in town left."

Duchovney Tuna

Worker #1: "When's the next shipment expected?"

Worker #2: "Not sure. Papers say noon but I doubt it'll be on time."

Worker #1: "You go to Vatz's Gentleman's Club yet?"

Worker #2: "Yeah. I practically live there at night."

Worker #1: "Doesn't your wife get mad?"

Worker #2: "We're kinda going through something right now."

Worker #1: "Oh yeah? That sucks."

Worker #2: "Yeah."

Worker #1: "Wanna grab something to eat?"

Worker #2: "$4.99 buffet?"

Worker #1: "[laughing] You're always thinking of food!"

The Mysterious Seven of Drewersville
A Crime Scene Inquiry Lab

K.J. Sukhu

Therapist A.M.

Therapist: "How are you feeling?"

????: "I'm stressed out. I need help doc."

Therapist: "Let's talk about your problems."

????: "I'm tired of talking. Just write a prescription."

Therapist: "You're already done? [sigh] Alright, I'll prescribe you one pack of these SSRI's."

Therapist P.M.

Therapist: "How are you feeling?"

????: "Not good."

Therapist: "Are you willing to talk today?"

????: "Maybe."

Therapist: "Let's talk about that girl…"

????: "Changed my mind. Can I go now? This is really starting to annoy me."

Therapist: "Fine, but are you taking your pills?"

????: "I ran out about a week ago."

Therapist: "You need to keep taking your medication even if you think you're fine. I don't want you hurting yourself again or injuring someone else."

????: *[angry brooding]*

Therapist: "Take this, a prescription for … a 'dopamine antagonist'."

The Mysterious Seven of Drewersville
A Crime Scene Inquiry Lab

K.J. Sukhu

Blood Analysis
Blood samples have been taken from as many people as possible

Blood samples can tell a lot about a person's health, what activities they've engaged in and other useful information that will aid an ongoing investigation

Person	Chemical Breakdown	
Mervin Padolski	BUN = 4 mg/dl CO_2 = 25 mEq/L Creatinine = 111 umol/L Glucose = 115 mg/dl 7-AminoFlunitrazepam = negative	Chloride = 100mEq/L BAC = 0.02% Cocaine = 0.02mg/L THC = 200 ng/mL Mercury = 4.5 ng/ml
Sherwin Makazaki	BUN = 12 mg/dl CO_2 = 27 mEq/L Creatinine = 106 umol/L Glucose = 74 mg/dl 7-AminoFlunitrazepam = negative	Chloride = 108 mEq/L BAC = 0.04% Cocaine = 0.00mg/L THC = 50 ng/mL Mercury = 2.5 ng/ml
Frank Duchovney	BUN =18 mg/dl CO_2 = 24 mEq/L Creatinine = 60 umol/L Glucose = 89 mg/dl 7-AminoFlunitrazepam = negative	Chloride = 106 mEq/L BAC = 0.00% Cocaine = 0.00mg/L THC = 50 ng/mL Mercury = 3 ng/ml
Adol Vice	BUN = 16 mg/dl CO_2 = 29 mEq/L Creatinine = 55 umol/L Glucose = 91 mg/dl 7-AminoFlunitrazepam = negative	Chloride = 100 mEq/L BAC = 0.01% Cocaine = 0.00mg/L THC = 00 ng/mL Mercury = 1 ng/ml
Jason Barret	BUN = 8 mg/dl CO_2 = 25 mEq/L Creatinine = 78 umol/L Glucose = 85 mg/dl 7-AminoFlunitrazepam = negative	Chloride = 105 mEq/L BAC = 0.02% Cocaine = 0.00mg/L THC = 50 ng/mL Mercury = 1.5 ng/ml
Sidney Vatz	BUN = 21 mg/dl CO_2 = 26 mEq/L Creatinine = 89 umol/L Glucose = 90 mg/dl 7-AminoFlunitrazepam = negative	Chloride = 100 mEq/L BAC = 0.06% Cocaine = 0.09mg/L THC = 150 ng/mL Mercury = 1 ng/ml
Jacob Franc	BUN = 8 mg/dl CO_2 = 28 mEq/L Creatinine = 59 umol/L Glucose = 105 mg/dl 7-AminoFlunitrazepam = negative	Chloride =105 mEq/L BAC = 0.10% Cocaine = 0.03mg/L THC =150 ng/mL Mercury = 1 ng/ml
Jeremy Toure (possible victim of a murder-suicide)	BUN = 21 mg/dl CO_2 = 29 mEq/L Creatinine = 61 umol/L Glucose = 89 mg/dl 7-AminoFlunitrazepam = positive	Chloride = 100 mEq/L BAC = 0.02% Cocaine = 0.00mg/L THC = 50 ng/mL Mercury = 1 ng/ml

IMPORTANT: This report contains proprietary and original material. Accordingly, this document may not be copied or released to third parties without consent.

The Mysterious Seven of Drewersville
A Crime Scene Inquiry Lab

K.J. Sukhu

Janson	BUN = 22.5 mg/dl CO_2 = 29 mEq/L Creatinine = 59 umol/L Glucose = 98 mg/dl 7-AminoFlunitrazepam = negative	Chloride = 100 mEq/L BAC = 0.04% Cocaine = 0.04mg/L THC = 150 ng/mL Mercury = 1 ng/ml
Nurse Claire	BUN = 20 mg/dl CO_2 = 29 mEq/L Creatinine = 89 umol/L Glucose = 90 mg/dl 7-AminoFlunitrazepam = negative	Chloride =100 mEq/L BAC = 0.01% Cocaine = 0.01mg/L THC = 50 ng/mL Mercury = 1 ng/ml
Bank Manager	BUN = 18 mg/dl CO_2 = 29 mEq/L Creatinine = 73 umol/L Glucose = 85 mg/dl 7-AminoFlunitrazepam = negative	Chloride = 100 mEq/L BAC = 0.00% Cocaine = 0.01mg/L THC = 50 ng/mL Mercury = 1 ng/ml
Kadri	BUN – 15 mg/dl CO_2 – 25 mEq/L Creatinine = 59 umol/L Glucose – 98 mg/dl 7-AminoFlunitrazepam = negative	Chloride = 100 mEq/L BAC = 0.03% Cocaine = 00mg/L THC = 0.00mg/L Mercury = 1.5 ng/ml
Duncan Mancini	No Blood Work Possible	
Dr. Allen	No Blood Work Possible	
Amy Droden	No Blood Work Possible	
Danny Arc	No Blood Work Possible	
Stacy Florense	No Blood Work Possible	
Jake Slow	No Blood Work Possible	
Anthony Plexi	No Blood Work Possible	
Alfred Gomez	No Blood Work Possible	
Mohamed Aljeer	No Blood Work Possible	
Brady Spark	No Blood Work Possible	
Victim 1: Burned body (Identity Unknown)	No Blood Work Possible	
Victim 3: A female body (Identity Unknown)	No Blood Work Possible	
Victim 4: (kidnapped)	No Blood Work Possible	
Victim 5: (kidnapped)	No Blood Work Possible	
Victim 6: Stacy McEnroe (coma)	BUN = 20 mg/dl CO_2 = 25 mEq/L Creatinine = 110 umol/L Glucose = 95 mg/dl 7-AminoFlunitrazepam = positive	Chloride =100 mEq/L BAC = 0.02% Cocaine = 0.00mg/L THC = 50 ng/mL Mercury = 1 ng/ml
Victim 7	BUN = 25 mg/dl CO_2 = 27 mEq/L Creatinine = 108 umol/L Glucose = 105 mg/dl 7-AminoFlunitrazepam = positive	Chloride = 121 mEq/L BAC = 0.08% Cocaine = 0.00mg/L THC = 50 ng/mL Mercury = 3.5 ng/ml

IMPORTANT: This report contains proprietary and original material. Accordingly, this document may not be copied or released to third parties without consent.

The Mysterious Seven of Drewersville
A Crime Scene Inquiry Lab

K.J. Sukhu

DNA Analysis
Using a restriction enzyme you will cut DNA into fragments

Authorities have collected DNA samples from various people throughout Drewersville. You will use a restriction enzyme to cut the DNA samples into bands. For detailed instructions on how to do this please refer to the Appendix section entitled "How to Cut DNA".

To cut the DNA you will use the restriction enzyme "Fay-KE". Look for the exact DNA pattern and cut only where instructed to (Figure 3-1). Remember that fragments are considered to be continuous (think of the 6 pieces as one long strand of DNA). Make sure you correctly identify all the areas to cut or your DNA bands will be incorrect.

Restriction Enzyme Fay-KE

```
              CG
              CG
              TA
             ———— Cut Here
              AT
              GC
  Figure 3-1  GC
```

Note: Instead of using a restriction enzyme that will produce "sticky ends", we will only consider "blunt ends" for this activity.

The Mysterious Seven of Drewersville
A Crime Scene Inquiry Lab

K.J. Sukhu

Mervin Padolski

1	2	3	4	5	6
C-G	G-C	A-T	A-T	T-A	C-G
C-G	T-A	C-G	A-T	T-A	C-G
T-A	T-A	A-T	G-C	G-C	T-A
A-T	G-C	A-T	A-T	C-G	A-T
G-C	C-G	A-T	C-G	A-T	G-C
G-C	A-T	G-C	A-T	C-G	G-C
G-C	C-G	C-G	C-G	A-T	T-A
T-A	A-T	G-C	C-G	A-T	G-C
T-A	A-T	T-A	T-A	A-T	C-G
G-C	A-T	T-A	A-T	G-C	A-T
C-G	G-C	A-T	G-C	T-A	C-G
A-T	C-G	C-G	G-C	T-A	A-T
A-T	G-C	A-T	A-T	A-T	A-T
A-T	T-A	A-T	A-T	C-G	A-T
G-C	T-A	A-T	A-T	A-T	G-C
C-G	G-C	G-C	G-C	A-T	T-A
A-T	C-G	C-G	C-G	A-T	T-A
T-A	G-C	G-C	G-C	G-C	A-T
G-C	T-A	T-A	T-A	C-G	C-G

Band #	DNA

Sherwin Makazaki

1	2	3	4	5	6
T-A	T-A	T-A	G-C	C-G	C-G
T-A	T-A	G-C	C-G	C-G	A-T
T-A	G-C	C-G	A-T	T-A	C-G
G-C	C-G	A-T	C-G	A-T	A-T
C-G	A-T	C-G	A-T	G-C	A-T
A-T	C-G	C-G	A-T	G-C	A-T
C-G	A-T	A-T	A-T	C-G	G-C
A-T	A-T	A-T	G-C	A-T	T-A
A-T	A-T	A-T	T-A	C-G	T-A
A-T	G-C	C-G	T-A	A-T	A-T
G-C	T-A	C-G	A-T	A-T	C-G
T-A	T-A	T-A	C-G	A-T	A-T
C-G	A-T	A-T	A-T	G-C	T-A
C-G	C-G	G-C	T-A	T-A	G-C
T-A	A-T	G-C	T-A	T-A	C-G
A-T	A-T	A-T	G-C	A-T	A-T
G-C	A-T	G-C	C-G	C-G	C-G
G-C	G-C	C-G	A-T	A-T	A-T
C-G	C-G	T-A	C-G	T-A	A-T

Band #	DNA

The Mysterious Seven of Drewersville
A Crime Scene Inquiry Lab

K.J. Sukhu

Frank Duchovney

1	2	3	4	5	6
A-T	A-T	T-A	T-A	T-A	C-G
G-C	G-C	T-A	A-T	T-A	C-G
T-A	T-A	G-C	C-G	G-C	T-A
T-A	T-A	C-G	A-T	C-G	A-T
A-T	C-G	A-T	T-A	A-T	G-C
C-G	C-G	C-G	T-A	C-G	G-C
A-T	T-A	A-T	G-C	A-T	A-T
T-A	A-T	A-T	C-G	C-G	C-G
T-A	G-C	A-T	A-T	C-G	A-T
G-C	G-C	G-C	C-G	T-A	A-T
C-G	C-G	T-A	A-T	A-T	A-T
A-T	A-T	T-A	C-G	G-C	G-C
C-G	A-T	A-T	A-T	G-C	C-G
A-T	A-T	C-G	A-T	A-T	C-G
C-G	G-C	A-T	A-T	G-C	T-A
A-T	C-G	A-T	G-C	A-T	A-T
A-T	A-T	A-T	A-T	G-C	G-C
A-T	C-G	G-C	G-C	C-G	G-C
G-C	A-T	C-G	C-G	C-G	A-T

Band #	DNA

Adol Vice

1	2	3	4	5	6
C-G	G-C	A-T	G-C	G-C	G-C
C-G	T-A	C-G	C-G	T-A	T-A
T-A	T-A	A-T	C-G	T-A	T-A
A-T	A-T	A-T	T-A	G-C	G-C
G-C	C-G	A-T	A-T	C-G	C-G
G-C	A-T	G-C	G-C	A-T	A-T
G-C	A-T	C-G	G-C	C-G	C-G
T-A	A-T	G-C	G-C	A-T	A-T
T-A	G-C	T-A	T-A	A-T	A-T
A-T	A-T	T-A	T-A	A-T	C-G
C-G	G-C	A-T	A-T	G-C	C-G
C-G	C-G	C-G	C-G	C-G	T-A
T-A	C-G	A-T	A-T	G-C	A-T
A-T	A-T	A-T	A-T	T-A	G-C
G-C	G-C	A-T	A-T	T-A	G-C
G-C	C-G	G-C	G-C	G-C	G-C
C-G	G-C	C-G	C-G	C-G	C-G
A-T	T-A	G-C	G-C	G-C	G-C
G-C	C-G	T-A	G-C	T-A	T-A

Band #	DNA

IMPORTANT: This report contains proprietary and original material. Accordingly, this document may not be copied or released to third parties without consent.

The Mysterious Seven of Drewersville
A Crime Scene Inquiry Lab

K.J. Sukhu

Jason Barret

1	2	3	4	5	6
T-A	G-C	C-G	G-C	A-T	G-C
G-C	T-A	C-G	C-G	C-G	C-G
C-G	T-A	T-A	A-T	A-T	A-T
G-C	G-C	A-T	C-G	A-T	C-G
T-A	C-G	G-C	A-T	A-T	C-G
C-G	A-T	G-C	A-T	G-C	C-G
C-G	C-G	C-G	A-T	C-G	T-A
T-A	A-T	A-T	G-C	C-G	A-T
A-T	A-T	A-T	T-A	T-A	G-C
G-C	A-T	A-T	T-A	A-T	G-C
G-C	G-C	G-C	A-T	G-C	C-G
A-T	C-G	C-G	C-G	G-C	A-T
C-G	G-C	G-C	A-T	A-T	A-T
A-T	T-A	T-A	T-A	T-A	A-T
A-T	T-A	G-C	T-A	T-A	G-C
A-T	G-C	C-G	G-C	G-C	T-A
G-C	C-G	G-C	C-G	C-G	T-A
C-G	G-C	T-A	A-T	T-A	A-T
T-A	T-A	C-G	C-G	G-C	C-G

Band #	DNA

Sidney Vatz

1	2	3	4	5	6
A-T	C-G	G-C	C-G	G-C	A-T
A-T	C-G	T-A	A-T	T-A	A-T
G-C	T-A	T-A	C-G	T-A	G-C
C-G	A-T	G-C	A-T	G-C	C-G
G-C	G-C	C-G	A-T	C-G	C-G
T-A	G-C	A-T	A-T	A-T	T-A
T-A	C-G	C-G	G-C	C-G	A-T
G-C	A-T	A-T	C-G	A-T	G-C
C-G	A-T	A-T	G-C	A-T	G-C
G-C	C-G	A-T	T-A	A-T	G-C
T-A	C-G	G-C	G-C	G-C	T-A
T-A	T-A	C-G	C-G	C-G	G-C
G-C	A-T	G-C	G-C	G-C	C-G
C-G	G-C	T-A	T-A	T-A	G-C
A-T	G-C	T-A	T-A	T-A	T-A
C-G	G-C	G-C	G-C	G-C	G-C
A-T	C-G	C-G	C-G	C-G	C-G
A-T	G-C	G-C	G-C	G-C	G-C
A-T	A-T	T-A	A-T	T-A	A-T

Band #	DNA

The Mysterious Seven of Drewersville
A Crime Scene Inquiry Lab

K.J. Sukhu

Jacob Franc

1	2	3	4	5	6
T-A	T-A	C-G	A-T	G-C	C-G
A-T	T-A	C-G	C-G	C-G	A-T
C-G	G-C	T-A	A-T	A-T	T-A
A-T	C-G	A-T	A-T	C-G	T-A
A-T	A-T	G-C	A-T	A-T	G-C
C-G	C-G	G-C	G-C	A-T	C-G
C-G	A-T	C-G	C-G	A-T	C-G
T-A	A-T	A-T	C-G	G-C	C-G
A-T	A-T	A-T	T-A	T-A	T-A
G-C	G-C	A-T	A-T	T-A	A-T
G-C	T-A	G-C	G-C	A-T	G-C
C-G	T-A	T-A	G-C	C-G	G-C
A-T	A-T	T-A	T-A	A-T	C-G
T-A	C-G	A-T	A-T	T-A	A-T
T-A	A-T	T-A	T-A	T-A	T-A
G-C	A-T	G-C	G-C	G-C	T-A
C-G	A-T	C-G	C-G	C-G	G-C
A-T	G-C	A-T	A-T	A-T	C-G
C-G	C-G	C-G	C-G	C-G	A-T

Band #	DNA

Doctor Allen

1	2	3	4	5	6
G-C	G-C	A-T	A-T	G-C	C-G
C-G	T-A	C-G	C-G	T-A	C-G
A-T	T-A	C-G	A-T	T-A	T-A
C-G	G-C	C-G	A-T	G-C	A-T
A-T	C-G	C-G	A-T	C-G	G-C
A-T	A-T	T-A	A-T	A-T	G-C
A-T	C-G	A-T	A-T	C-G	C-G
G-C	C-G	G-C	A-T	A-T	A-T
T-A	G-C	G-C	G-C	A-T	A-T
T-A	T-A	C-G	C-G	A-T	A-T
A-T	C-G	A-T	C-G	G-C	G-C
C-G	C-G	C-G	T-A	C-G	T-A
A-T	T-A	A-T	A-T	G-C	T-A
T-A	A-T	A-T	G-C	T-A	A-T
T-A	G-C	A-T	G-C	T-A	C-G
G-C	G-C	G-C	T-A	G-C	A-T
C-G	T-A	C-G	G-C	C-G	T-A
A-T	T-A	G-C	C-G	G-C	T-A
C-G	G-C	T-A	G-C	T-A	G-C

Band #	DNA

The Mysterious Seven of Drewersville
A Crime Scene Inquiry Lab

K.J. Sukhu

Amy Droden

1	2	3	4	5	6
G-C	G-C	G-C	G-C	G-C	A-T
T-A	T-A	T-A	T-A	C-G	C-G
T-A	T-A	T-A	T-A	A-T	A-T
G-C	G-C	G-C	G-C	C-G	T-A
C-G	C-G	C-G	C-G	A-T	C-G
A-T	A-T	A-T	A-T	A-T	C-G
C-G	C-G	C-G	C-G	A-T	T-A
C-G	C-G	A-T	C-G	G-C	A-T
T-A	T-A	A-T	T-A	T-A	G-C
A-T	A-T	A-T	A-T	T-A	G-C
G-C	G-C	G-C	G-C	A-T	T-A
G-C	G-C	C-G	G-C	C-G	T-A
C-G	T-A	G-C	A-T	A-T	A-T
G-C	G-C	T-A	C-G	T-A	C-G
T-A	C-G	T-A	A-T	T-A	A-T
C-G	G-C	G-C	T-A	G-C	T-A
G-C	T-A	C-G	T-A	C-G	T-A
T-A	G-C	G-C	G-C	A-T	C-G
C-G	C-G	T-A	C-G	C-G	A-T

Band #	DNA

Danny Arc

1	2	3	4	5	6
G-C	G-C	C-G	G-C	G-C	G-C
C-G	T-A	C-G	C-G	T-A	C-G
G-C	T-A	T-A	C-G	T-A	A-T
T-A	G-C	A-T	T-A	G-C	C-G
C-G	C-G	G-C	A-T	C-G	A-T
C-G	A-T	G-C	G-C	A-T	A-T
T-A	C-G	A-T	G-C	C-G	A-T
A-T	A-T	C-G	A-T	A-T	G-C
G-C	A-T	A-T	G-C	T-A	T-A
G-C	A-T	A-T	T-A	C-G	T-A
C-G	G-C	A-T	T-A	C-G	A-T
G-C	C-G	G-C	A-T	T-A	C-G
T-A	G-C	T-A	C-G	A-T	A-T
T-A	T-A	T-A	A-T	G-C	T-A
G-C	T-A	A-T	T-A	G-C	T-A
C-G	G-C	C-G	T-A	C-G	G-C
C-G	C-G	A-T	G-C	A-T	C-G
A-T	G-C	T-A	A-T	T-A	A-T
C-G	T-A	G-C	T-A	T-A	C-G

Band #	DNA

The Mysterious Seven of Drewersville
A Crime Scene Inquiry Lab

K.J. Sukhu

Stacy Florense

1	2	3	4	5	6
A-T	C-G	A-T	G-C	G-C	G-C
G-C	C-G	A-T	T-A	C-G	C-G
G-C	T-A	G-C	T-A	A-T	A-T
A-T	A-T	G-C	G-C	C-G	C-G
C-G	G-C	C-G	C-G	C-G	A-T
C-G	G-C	C-G	A-T	T-A	A-T
T-A	A-T	T-A	C-G	A-T	A-T
A-T	C-G	A-T	A-T	G-C	G-C
G-C	A-T	G-C	A-T	G-C	T-A
G-C	A-T	G-C	A-T	T-A	T-A
T-A	A-T	A-T	G-C	A-T	A-T
A-T	G-C	A-T	C-G	C-G	C-G
C-G	C-G	G-C	G-C	A-T	A-T
A-T	G-C	C-G	T-A	T-A	T-A
T-A	T-A	G-C	T-A	T-A	T-A
T-A	T-A	T-A	G-C	G-C	G-C
G-C	G-C	T-A	C-G	C-G	C-G
C-G	C-G	T-A	G-C	T-A	A-T
T-A	G-C	G-C	T-A	G-C	C-G

Band #	DNA

Jake Slow

1	2	3	4	5	6
G-C	G-C	T-A	G-C	G-C	G-C
T-A	T-A	C-G	C-G	T-A	T-A
T-A	T-A	C-G	A-T	T-A	T-A
G-C	G-C	T-A	C-G	G-C	G-C
C-G	C-G	A-T	A-T	C-G	C-G
A-T	A-T	G-C	A-T	A-T	C-G
C-G	C-G	G-C	A-T	C-G	T-A
C-G	A-T	G-C	G-C	A-T	A-T
T-A	A-T	T-A	T-A	A-T	G-C
A-T	A-T	T-A	T-A	A-T	G-C
G-C	G-C	G-C	A-T	G-C	T-A
G-C	C-G	C-G	C-G	C-G	T-A
C-G	G-C	A-T	A-T	G-C	A-T
A-T	T-A	C-G	T-A	T-A	C-G
C-G	T-A	A-T	T-A	T-A	A-T
A-T	G-C	A-T	G-C	G-C	T-A
A-T	C-G	A-T	C-G	C-G	T-A
A-T	G-C	G-C	A-T	G-C	G-C
G-C	T-A	C-G	C-G	T-A	C-G

Band #	DNA

IMPORTANT: This report contains proprietary and original material. Accordingly, this document may not be copied or released to third parties without consent.

The Mysterious Seven of Drewersville
A Crime Scene Inquiry Lab

K.J. Sukhu

Anthony Plexi

1	2	3	4	5	6
G-C	A-T	G-C	G-C	G-C	G-C
C-G	A-T	T-A	C-G	C-G	C-G
A-T	G-C	T-A	A-T	C-G	A-T
C-G	C-G	G-C	C-G	T-A	C-G
A-T	G-C	C-G	A-T	A-T	A-T
A-T	T-A	A-T	A-T	G-C	A-T
C-G	T-A	C-G	A-T	G-C	A-T
C-G	G-C	A-T	G-C	G-C	G-C
T-A	C-G	A-T	T-A	T-A	T-A
A-T	G-C	A-T	T-A	T-A	T-A
G-C	T-A	G-C	A-T	A-T	A-T
G-C	A-T	C-G	C-G	C-G	C-G
A-T	C-G	G-C	A-T	A-T	C-G
G-C	A-T	T-A	T-A	A-T	C-G
T-A	A-T	T-A	T-A	G-C	T-A
G-C	A-T	G-C	G-C	T-A	A-T
C-G	G-C	C-G	C-G	T-A	G-C
G-C	C-G	G-C	A-T	A-T	G-C
T-A	G-C	T-A	C-G	C-G	A-T

Band #	DNA

Alfred Gomez

1	2	3	4	5	6
G-C	G-C	C-G	G-C	C-G	A-T
C-G	T-A	G-C	C-G	C-G	A-T
A-T	T-A	T-A	A-T	T-A	G-C
C-G	G-C	T-A	C-G	A-T	C-G
A-T	C-G	G-C	A-T	G-C	G-C
A-T	A-T	C-G	A-T	G-C	T-A
A-T	C-G	G-C	A-T	G-C	T-A
A-T	A-T	C-G	G-C	C-G	G-C
A-T	A-T	G-C	T-A	G-C	C-G
A-T	A-T	T-A	T-A	T-A	G-C
G-C	G-C	C-G	A-T	A-T	T-A
C-G	C-G	C-G	C-G	C-G	A-T
C-G	G-C	T-A	A-T	A-T	C-G
T-A	T-A	A-T	T-A	A-T	A-T
A-T	T-A	G-C	T-A	A-T	A-T
G-C	G-C	G-C	G-C	G-C	A-T
G-C	C-G	G-C	C-G	C-G	G-C
C-G	G-C	T-A	A-T	A-T	C-G
A-T	T-A	T-A	C-G	C-G	G-C

Band #	DNA

The Mysterious Seven of Drewersville
A Crime Scene Inquiry Lab

K.J. Sukhu

Mohamed Aljeer

1	2	3	4	5	6
T-A	G-C	G-C	G-C	A-T	G-C
T-A	C-G	C-G	T-A	A-T	C-G
A-T	A-T	A-T	T-A	G-C	C-G
C-G	C-G	C-G	G-C	C-G	T-A
A-T	A-T	A-T	C-G	G-C	A-T
T-A	A-T	C-G	A-T	T-A	G-C
C-G	A-T	C-G	C-G	T-A	G-C
C-G	G-C	T-A	A-T	G-C	A-T
T-A	T-A	A-T	A-T	C-G	C-G
A-T	T-A	G-C	A-T	G-C	A-T
G-C	A-T	G-C	G-C	T-A	A-T
G-C	C-G	G-C	C-G	A-T	A-T
C-G	A-T	C-G	G-C	C-G	G-C
G-C	T-A	G-C	T-A	A-T	C-G
T-A	T-A	T-A	T-A	A-T	G-C
A-T	G-C	A-T	G-C	A-T	T-A
C-G	C-G	C-G	C-G	G-C	T-A
A-T	A-T	A-T	G-C	C-G	G-C
A-T	C-G	A-T	T-A	G-C	C-G

Band #	DNA

Jeremy Toure

1	2	3	4	5	6
A-T	G-C	G-C	C-G	A-T	G-C
G-C	C-G	T-A	G-C	C-G	C-G
T-A	A-T	T-A	T-A	A-T	A-T
T-A	C-G	G-C	T-A	C-G	C-G
A-T	A-T	C-G	G-C	C-G	A-T
C-G	A-T	A-T	C-G	T-A	A-T
A-T	A-T	C-G	C-G	A-T	A-T
T-A	G-C	A-T	T-A	G-C	G-C
C-G	T-A	A-T	A-T	G-C	C-G
C-G	T-A	A-T	G-C	T-A	C-G
T-A	A-T	G-C	G-C	T-A	T-A
A-T	C-G	C-G	A-T	G-C	A-T
G-C	A-T	G-C	G-C	C-G	G-C
G-C	T-A	T-A	T-A	A-T	G-C
A-T	T-A	T-A	T-A	C-G	T-A
C-G	G-C	G-C	A-T	A-T	G-C
A-T	C-G	C-G	C-G	A-T	C-G
T-A	A-T	G-C	A-T	A-T	G-C
T-A	C-G	T-A	T-A	G-C	T-A

Band #	DNA

IMPORTANT: This report contains proprietary and original material. Accordingly, this document may not be copied or released to third parties without consent.

The Mysterious Seven of Drewersville
A Crime Scene Inquiry Lab

K.J. Sukhu

Stacy McEnroe

1	2	3	4	5	6
G-C	G-C	G-C	G-C	G-C	G-C
C-G	C-G	T-A	T-A	T-A	T-A
A-T	A-T	T-A	C-G	T-A	T-A
C-G	C-G	G-C	C-G	G-C	G-C
A-T	A-T	C-G	T-A	C-G	C-G
A-T	C-G	A-T	A-T	A-T	A-T
A-T	C-G	C-G	G-C	C-G	C-G
G-C	T-A	A-T	G-C	C-G	A-T
T-A	A-T	A-T	A-T	T-A	A-T
T-A	G-C	C-G	G-C	A-T	A-T
A-T	G-C	C-G	T-A	G-C	G-C
C-G	A-T	T-A	T-A	G-C	C-G
A-T	A-T	A-T	A-T	G-C	G-C
T-A	G-C	G-C	C-G	T-A	T-A
T-A	C-G	G-C	A-T	T-A	T-A
G-C	G-C	G-C	T-A	A-T	G-C
C-G	T-A	T-A	T-A	C-G	C-G
A-T	T-A	T-A	G-C	A-T	G-C
C-G	T-A	G-C	T-A	T-A	T-A

Band #	DNA

Duncan Mancini

1	2	3	4	5	6
G-C	G-C	G-C	T-A	T-A	T-A
T-A	T-A	T-A	G-C	T-A	T-A
T-A	T-A	T-A	C-G	G-C	G-C
G-C	G-C	G-C	C-G	C-G	C-G
C-G	C-G	C-G	T-A	A-T	A-T
G-C	A-T	A-T	A-T	G-C	G-C
T-A	C-G	C-G	G-C	C-G	C-G
C-G	A-T	A-T	G-C	C-G	C-G
C-G	A-T	A-T	T-A	C-G	T-A
T-A	A-T	C-G	A-T	T-A	A-T
A-T	G-C	C-G	G-C	A-T	G-C
G-C	C-G	T-A	C-G	G-C	C-G
G-C	G-C	A-T	G-C	G-C	G-C
A-T	T-A	G-C	T-A	T-A	T-A
C-G	T-A	G-C	T-A	T-A	T-A
A-T	G-C	C-G	G-C	G-C	G-C
A-T	C-G	G-C	C-G	C-G	C-G
A-T	G-C	T-A	G-C	G-C	G-C
G-C	T-A	T-A	T-A	T-A	T-A

Band #	DNA

The Mysterious Seven of Drewersville K.J. Sukhu
A Crime Scene Inquiry Lab

Andrew Gandolfini

1	2	3	4	5	6
G-C	C-G	T-A	C-G	T-A	T-A
T-A	G-C	C-G	G-C	T-A	T-A
T-A	T-A	C-G	T-A	C-G	G-C
G-C	A-T	T-A	A-T	C-G	C-G
C-G	G-C	A-T	G-C	T-A	A-T
A-T	C-G	G-C	C-G	A-T	G-C
C-G	C-G	G-C	A-T	G-C	C-G
A-T	C-G	A-T	C-G	G-C	G-C
A-T	T-A	A-T	C-G	A-T	T-A
A-T	A-T	A-T	T-A	A-T	A-T
G-C	G-C	G-C	A-T	A-T	G-C
C-G	G-C	C-G	G-C	G-C	C-G
G-C	A-T	G-C	G-C	C-G	G-C
T-A	G-C	T-A	T-A	G-C	T-A
T-A	C-G	T-A	T-A	T-A	T-A
G-C	G-C	G-C	G-C	T-A	G-C
C-G	T-A	G-C	C-G	G-C	C-G
G-C	T-A	T-A	G-C	G-C	G-C
T-A	G-C	C-G	T-A	T-A	T-A

Band #	DNA

Brady Spark

1	2	3	4	5	6
T-A	G-C	T-A	A-T	G-C	G-C
G-C	C-G	T-A	G-C	C-G	T-A
C-G	A-T	G-C	C-G	A-T	T-A
C-G	C-G	C-G	G-C	C-G	G-C
T-A	A-T	A-T	T-A	A-T	C-G
A-T	C-G	G-C	T-A	A-T	A-T
G-C	C-G	C-G	G-C	A-T	C-G
G-C	T-A	G-C	C-G	G-C	A-T
A-T	A-T	T-A	G-C	T-A	A-T
A-T	G-C	A-T	C-G	T-A	A-T
A-T	G-C	G-C	G-C	A-T	G-C
G-C	G-C	C-G	C-G	C-G	C-G
T-A	C-G	G-C	C-G	A-T	G-C
T-A	A-T	T-A	T-A	T-A	T-A
A-T	G-C	T-A	A-T	T-A	T-A
C-G	C-G	G-C	G-C	G-C	G-C
A-T	G-C	C-G	G-C	C-G	C-G
T-A	T-A	G-C	A-T	A-T	G-C
T-A	A-T	T-A	C-G	C-G	T-A

Band #	DNA

The Mysterious Seven of Drewersville
A Crime Scene Inquiry Lab

K.J. Sukhu

Janson

1	2	3	4	5	6
G-C	T-A	T-A	G-C	A-T	T-A
C-G	T-A	T-A	C-G	C-G	A-T
C-G	G-C	C-G	A-T	C-G	C-G
T-A	C-G	C-G	C-G	C-G	A-T
A-T	A-T	T-A	A-T	T-A	T-A
G-C	G-C	A-T	A-T	A-T	T-A
G-C	C-G	G-C	A-T	G-C	A-T
T-A	G-C	G-C	G-C	G-C	C-G
A-T	T-A	A-T	T-A	T-A	C-G
C-G	A-T	C-G	T-A	A-T	C-G
A-T	G-C	T-A	A-T	C-G	T-A
T-A	C-G	A-T	C-G	A-T	A-T
T-A	G-C	C-G	A-T	T-A	G-C
G-C	T-A	A-T	T-A	T-A	G-C
T-A	T-A	T-A	T-A	T-A	T-A
T-A	G-C	T-A	G-C	G-C	G-C
G-C	C-G	A-T	C-G	C-G	C-G
C-G	G-C	C-G	A-T	A-T	A-T
T-A	T-A	G-C	C-G	T-A	C-G

Band #	DNA

Nurse Claire

1	2	3	4	5	6
T-A	T-A	T-A	G-C	A-T	T-A
T-A	T-A	T-A	C-G	C-G	A-T
A-T	G-C	C-G	A-T	C-G	C-G
C-G	C-G	C-G	C-G	C-G	A-T
A-T	A-T	T-A	A-T	T-A	T-A
T-A	G-C	A-T	A-T	A-T	T-A
T-A	C-G	G-C	C-G	G-C	A-T
G-C	G-C	G-C	C-G	G-C	C-G
C-G	T-A	A-T	T-A	T-A	C-G
A-T	A-T	C-G	A-T	A-T	C-G
C-G	G-C	T-A	G-C	C-G	T-A
G-C	C-G	A-T	G-C	A-T	A-T
T-A	G-C	C-G	A-T	T-A	G-C
T-A	T-A	C-G	T-A	T-A	G-C
G-C	T-A	T-A	T-A	T-A	T-A
C-G	G-C	A-T	G-C	G-C	G-C
G-C	C-G	G-C	C-G	C-G	C-G
T-A	G-C	G-C	A-T	A-T	A-T
G-C	T-A	G-C	C-G	T-A	C-G

Band #	DNA

IMPORTANT: This report contains proprietary and original material. Accordingly, this document may not be copied or released to third parties without consent.

The Mysterious Seven of Drewersville
A Crime Scene Inquiry Lab

K.J. Sukhu

Bank Manager

1	2	3	4	5	6
C-G	A-T	A-T	G-C	C-G	G-C
C-G	A-T	C-G	C-G	G-C	C-G
T-A	T-A	C-G	A-T	T-A	A-T
A-T	T-A	T-A	C-G	A-T	C-G
G-C	G-C	A-T	A-T	A-T	A-T
G-C	C-G	G-C	A-T	T-A	A-T
T-A	A-T	G-C	A-T	T-A	A-T
G-C	C-G	A-T	G-C	G-C	G-C
C-G	C-G	G-C	C-G	C-G	C-G
G-C	G-C	C-G	G-C	C-G	G-C
C-G	T-A	A-T	T-A	T-A	T-A
A-T	A-T	C-G	A-T	A-T	A-T
A-T	C-G	C-G	A-T	G-C	A-T
A-T	C-G	G-C	T-A	G-C	T-A
G-C	T-A	T-A	T-A	T-A	T-A
C-G	A-T	T-A	G-C	G-C	G-C
G-C	G-C	G-C	C-G	C-G	C-G
T-A	G-C	T-A	A-T	G-C	A-T
A-T	C-G	A-T	C-G	T-A	C-G

Band #	DNA

Kadri

1	2	3	4	5	6
A-T	G-C	A-T	A-T	T-A	C-G
A-T	T-A	C-G	A-T	T-A	C-G
G-C	T-A	A-T	G-C	G-C	T-A
C-G	G-C	A-T	A-T	C-G	A-T
G-C	C-G	A-T	C-G	A-T	G-C
T-A	A-T	G-C	A-T	C-G	G-C
G-C	C-G	C-G	C-G	A-T	T-A
T-A	A-T	G-C	C-G	A-T	G-C
T-A	A-T	T-A	T-A	A-T	C-G
G-C	A-T	T-A	A-T	G-C	A-T
C-G	G-C	A-T	G-C	T-A	C-G
A-T	C-G	C-G	G-C	T-A	A-T
A-T	G-C	A-T	A-T	A-T	A-T
A-T	T-A	A-T	A-T	C-G	A-T
G-C	T-A	A-T	A-T	A-T	G-C
C-G	G-C	G-C	G-C	A-T	T-A
A-T	C-G	C-G	C-G	A-T	T-A
T-A	G-C	G-C	G-C	G-C	A-T
G-C	T-A	T-A	T-A	C-G	C-G

Band #	DNA

IMPORTANT: This report contains proprietary and original material. Accordingly, this document may not be copied or released to third parties without consent.

The Mysterious Seven of Drewersville
A Crime Scene Inquiry Lab

K.J. Sukhu

Forest Ranger

1	2	3	4	5	6
C-G	A-T	A-T	G-C	C-G	G-C
A-T	G-C	A-T	C-G	G-C	C-G
C-G	G-C	G-C	A-T	T-A	A-T
C-G	T-A	C-G	C-G	A-T	C-G
G-C	C-G	G-C	A-T	A-T	C-G
T-A	C-G	T-A	A-T	T-A	T-A
T-A	T-A	A-T	A-T	T-A	A-T
G-C	A-T	A-T	G-C	G-C	G-C
C-G	G-C	G-C	C-G	C-G	G-C
G-C	G-C	C-G	C-G	A-T	G-C
C-G	T-A	A-T	C-G	C-G	T-A
A-T	A-T	C-G	T-A	C-G	A-T
A-T	A-T	C-G	A-T	G-C	A-T
A-T	T-A	G-C	G-C	T-A	T-A
G-C	T-A	T-A	G-C	T-A	T-A
C-G	T-A	T-A	G-C	G-C	G-C
C-G	T-A	G-C	C-G	C-G	C-G
C-G	G-C	T-A	A-T	G-C	A-T
T-A	C-G	A-T	C-G	T-A	C-G

Band #	DNA

Condo Developer

1	2	3	4	5	6
A-T	C-G	A-T	C-G	G-C	C-G
C-G	C-G	A-T	G-C	C-G	C-G
A-T	T-A	T-A	T-A	G-C	T-A
A-T	A-T	C-G	A-T	T-A	A-T
A-T	G-C	C-G	A-T	A-T	G-C
G-C	G-C	T-A	T-A	A-T	G-C
C-G	T-A	A-T	T-A	T-A	A-T
G-C	G-C	G-C	G-C	T-A	G-C
T-A	C-G	G-C	C-G	C-G	C-G
A-T	A-T	C-G	A-T	A-T	G-C
A-T	A-T	A-T	C-G	A-T	T-A
T-A	A-T	C-G	G-C	A-T	A-T
T-A	T-A	C-G	C-G	C-G	A-T
G-C	T-A	G-C	A-T	C-G	T-A
C-G	G-C	T-A	C-G	T-A	T-A
G-C	C-G	T-A	G-C	A-T	G-C
C-G	A-T	G-C	C-G	G-C	C-G
A-T	C-G	T-A	A-T	G-C	A-T
C-G	G-C	A-T	C-G	T-A	C-G

Band #	DNA

The Mysterious Seven of Drewersville
A Crime Scene Inquiry Lab

K.J. Sukhu

Objects of Significance Found
The bodies of the victims and other pieces of evidence have been inspected

DNA has been recovered from the crime scene. This will go a long way into 1) identifying who the actual victims are and 2) figuring out who may be the murderer(s).

Victim 1

A burnt body was found in a small ditch in the forest behind the town's baseball stadium. Semen was found on the body.

The best sample of DNA found at the scene of the crime yielded the following bands.

Band	Mixed DNA
43	
39	
38	
32	
29	
25	
16	
15	
13	
12	
10	
8	
4	

Victim 2

A body was found buried in a grave. The body (a male) was partially burned.

The body is thought to be that of Jeremy Toure (a victim of a possible murder-suicide).

Band	Mixed DNA
60	
54	
38	
33	
26	
25	
24	
17	
12	
11	
10	
8	
4	

IMPORTANT: This report contains proprietary and original material. Accordingly, this document may not be copied or released to third parties without consent.

The Mysterious Seven of Drewersville
A Crime Scene Inquiry Lab

K.J. Sukhu

Jacob Franc

Although not classified as a victim, Jacob Franc's body was burned and suffered what is thought to be a self inflicted gunshot wound.

Band	Mixed DNA
39	☐
38	☐
33	☐
25	☐
10	☐
8	☐
4	☐

Victim 3

A female body was found burned and dumped in the bottom of the lake in the park.

Band	Mixed DNA
70	☐
39	☐
38	☐
37	☐
35	☐
32	☐
29	☐
25	☐
23	☐
22	☐
15	☐
13	☐
9	☐
8	☐
7	☐
4	☐

The Mysterious Seven of Drewersville
A Crime Scene Inquiry Lab

Victim 6 (Stacy McEnroe)

Stacy has suffered severe burns and remains in a coma. This was the mixed DNA recovered from her purse (which was untouched by the fire).

Band	Mixed DNA
63	☐
44	☐
33	☐
32	☐
29	☐
27	☐
23	☐
17	☐
16	☐
12	☐
8	☐
3	☐

Victim 7

A partially burned body was dumped and left underneath the docks. DNA was extracted from the body. Collecting the DNA from this body was difficult and may not be very accurate.

Band	Mixed DNA
71	☐
35	☐
30	☐
15	☐
10	☐
9	☐
7	☐
4	☐
3	☐

The Mysterious Seven of Drewersville
A Crime Scene Inquiry Lab

K.J. Sukhu

Letter 1

This was the first letter sent to the police. DNA samples recovered revealed absolutely no DNA.

The letter read: "Leave it alone. Don't press and I'll stop.

Band	Mixed DNA

Letter 2

This was the second letter sent to the authorities. It arrived roughly a week and half after the first letter.

The letter read: "I'm having so much fun… aren't you?"

Band	Mixed DNA
63	
60	
38	
33	
32	
19	
16	
14	
12	
9	
3	

Letter 3

This was the third letter sent to the authorities, five days after the second letter was recieved by the police.

The letter read: "I'm not such a bad guy…you know?"

Band	Mixed DNA
63	
38	
36	
32	
19	
16	
12	
9	
3	

The Mysterious Seven of Drewersville
A Crime Scene Inquiry Lab

K.J. Sukhu

Suicide Letter

The suicide letter was recovered at Jacob's apartment. DNA was recoverd from this letter and has since been accidentally destroyed.

Band	Mixed DNA
54	
44	
38	
33	
25	
24	
17	
12	
11	
10	
8	

The Mysterious Seven of Drewersville   K.J. Sukhu
A Crime Scene Inquiry Lab

What Do I Hand In?
After going through all the evidence you should come up with a solid case

The murderer(s) should be identified, their motives as well as their victims. Cause of death should be revealed. All evidence to support your claims should also be presented.

1. Students will provide a "web" to visually connect the murderer(s) to their victim(s).

The web should also include possible motives and/or possible connections to other victims (refer to example Figure 3-2).

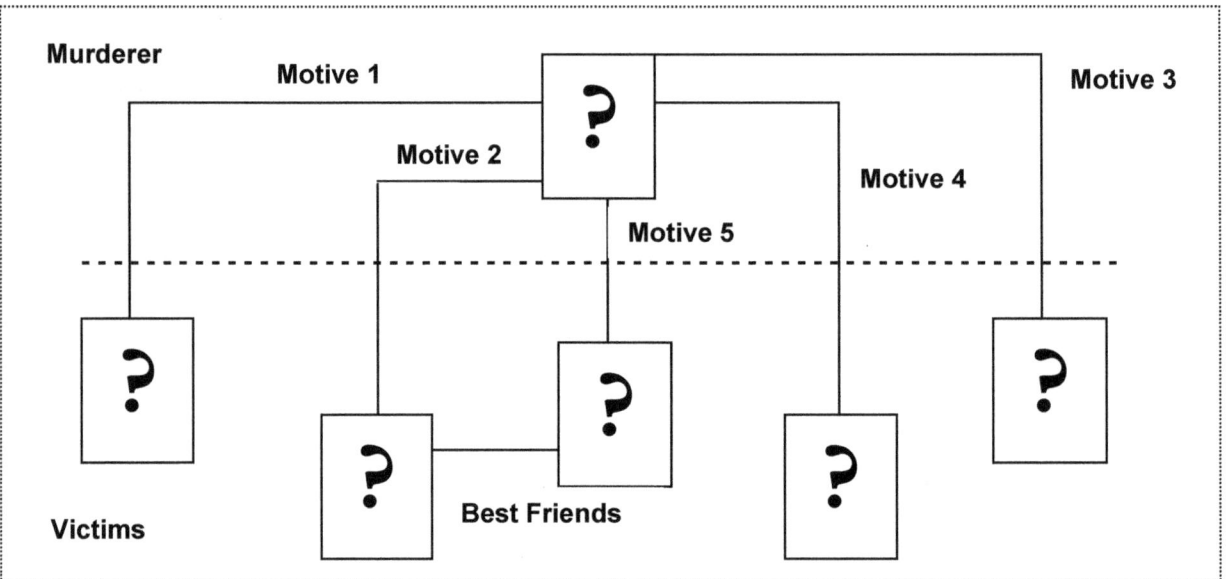

Figure 3-2

2. To accompany the visual relationship web, a detailed profile of the murderer(s) must be given.

This profile should include the following:
- A full explanation of the motive behind the murders.
- All available evidence that supports your accusation.

This may be written in paragraph form or may be put into a format such as the one shown in Figure 3-3.

The Mysterious Seven of Drewersville   K.J. Sukhu
A Crime Scene Inquiry Lab

3. A profile of each victim should be completed (Figure 3-4).

Profile

- Murderer: _____
- Age: _____
- Gender: _____

Victim: _____

Motive: _____

Evidence: _____

Figure 3-3

Profile

- Victim: _____
- Age: _____
- Gender: _____

Murdered By: _____

Cause of Death: _____

Evidence: _____

Figure 3-4

4. A map of Drewersville will be completed (you may use the next page).

The Mysterious Seven of Drewersville
A Crime Scene Inquiry Lab

K.J. Sukhu

Map of Drewersville

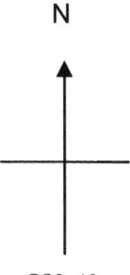

IMPORTANT: This report contains proprietary and original material. Accordingly, this document may not be copied or released to third parties without consent.

The Dolphin Hotel Murders

A case study in which victims, murderers and accomplices need to be identified using blood samples, DNA and reports

This is an advanced case study lab

The Dolphin Hotel Murders
A Forensic Crime Scene Inquiry Lab

K.J. Sukhu

Background

One of the country's largest cities, Izalith (in the region of New Londo), has recently been rocked by several natural disasters one after the other. Izalith has suffered tornadoes, typhoons and never-ending rain. The storms started in early July and have not let up. It's now winter and the situation is dire. The storms were never expected to be as impactful as they were, so it has taken citizens, government and rescue support by surprise. No one was equipped to deal with the unexpected weather. Homes have been destroyed. People have been stranded and food, clothes and clean drinking water are at a premium. Many people have taken shelter in hotels, hostels, and anywhere with space to house people from the harsh conditions. Power was knocked out of the city after the first storm. It was temporarily brought back in the form of rolling blackouts, but once again is completely out. Torrential downpours prevented any rescue attempts early on and extreme flooding engulfed the city. Now the water has turned into ice. It is almost impossible for a full scale rescue effort to take place. The weather is unbearably cold and snow has blanketed the city. The government has issued a state of emergency and essentially, anarchy rules. The streets that aren't flooded appear desolate but continue to be controlled by gangs. Graffiti is posted all over city buildings. Blockades have been set up all over the city. Some of these blockades were erected by gangs to maintain their territory, while others were set up by citizens in order to protect themselves.

One last refuge is a hotel that is almost impossible to enter anymore, the Dolphin. The Dolphin is one of the oldest and more regal hotels. Before the storm, it was considered a five star hotel. Each floor could have been regarded as an independent hotel in itself as each floor was equipped with state of the art facilities. The hotel was designed so that guests would never have to leave their floor other than to leave the hotel. Now, it wouldn't even be fit to be called dilapidated. The first few floors have been barricaded so that no one can leave nor enter. Most of the floors have been destroyed as a result of looting and harsh weather conditions. The building offers almost no protection from the outside elements, thus rendering most of the hotel uninhabitable during the cold winter season. There is however, one floor that has maintained its living conditions, Floor 14.

Hotel Information

Many people believe the number 13 to be an unlucky number. In an attempt to lessen superstitions, most older hotels omit floor "13"; and instead, skip to 14. However, for the Dolphin it was not enough to lessen superstitions, and so, while the hotel enjoyed a 90% occupancy rate, the 14th floor was rarely booked. Consequently, the manager of the hotel

The Dolphin Hotel Murders
A Forensic Crime Scene Inquiry Lab

K.J. Sukhu

decided to move storage equipment to the 14th floor. The floor had several hand cranked and gas powered generators. It also housed many of the water, pop and snack foods that one would find in the "mini-bars" of the hotel rooms. When the looting hit, the manager was quick to board up the windows and secure the floor before looters could get to the supplies. The occupancy of the floor is now at 41 individuals and dropping.

So far, the federal government has come under immense pressure domestically for their almost non-existent reaction to the crisis. There is sure to be a public inquiry after everything settles and so the government wants this situation handled swiftly and with care. To make matters worse, before the chaos hit there was an international conference on climate change. Many delegates from all over the world attended the conference. Most left Izalith before the first storm trapped everyone but there are some delegates who didn't get out. Particularly, there are three delegates who are unaccounted for; a Russian ambassador, a North Korean ambassador and an Iranian ambassador. The government doesn't need any more scrutiny, especially international scrutiny. As a result, the government called in a survey team to assess the situation. Among the team were scientists to survey the damage and collect data. However, no one could foresee the problems that started to occur in the Dolphin. After about a week, the team gathered the data and sent it to a secondary location with a recommendation to hold off on the rescue attempt until the whole story had been solved. It seems that life in the Dolphin has very shady undercurrents to it. Several bodies have been uncovered. With the entrances and exits sealed, only people within the Dolphin could have committed the murders. However, on their way out, the team was hit by another storm and are now missing (which isn't your concern). So now all that remains is the fragmented information that the team collected. You must use the data provided to figure out the identity of the victims and the murderer(s).

To Help You Solve the Case You Will Have the Following Information	1. **Dead Bodies Profile List** - You will have to change and update this list as you go through the evidence. 2. **Character Profile List** - Based on the information gathered, no one knows who has been murdered or who is a murderer. It's up to a keen team to figure it out. 3. **Geographical Landscape/Map of Floor 14** - Figuring out the layout of the Dolphin Hotel along with the

The Dolphin Hotel Murders
A Forensic Crime Scene Inquiry Lab

K.J. Sukhu

occupants of each room is very important to the case. You will use this to situate each occupant in their appropriate room.

4. **Interview with Residents**
   - People talk a lot. Let this aid you in your quest to uncover the truth.

5. **Statements Taken From Associates Outside the Dolphin**
   - Knowing who someone was before they went into the Dolphin may help figure out what role they might have played during the chaos.

6. **Blood Analysis**
   - Looking at people's blood samples might seem useless, but some investigation into what the samples mean might be fruitful.

7. **Objects of Significance Recovered**
   - The DNA found on the bodies will be invaluable to solving the case.

8. **DNA Analysis**
   - The DNA you "cut" will be needed to compare to the DNA found on the victims.

The Dolphin Hotel Murders
A Forensic Crime Scene Inquiry Lab

K.J. Sukhu

Dead Body Profiles List
The following bodies were found in the Dolphin Hotel

This list provides descriptions of victims who have been discovered in the Dolphin Hotel. Their bodies have not yet been identified. Please figure out the identities of the dead victims.

Victim 1
Description: Body severely burned.
Gender: Female
Identity: Unknown

Victim 2
Description: Portions of body missing.
Gender: Male
Identity: Unknown

Victim 3
Description: Face removed.
Gender: Male
Identity: Unknown

Victim 4
Description: Rotting corpse.
Gender: Male
Identity: Unknown

Victim 5
Description: Died from internal bleeding.
Gender: Male
Identity: Unknown

Victim 6
Description: Severely abused.
Gender: Male
Identity: Unknown

IMPORTANT: This report contains proprietary and original material. Accordingly, this document may not be copied or released to third parties without consent.

The Dolphin Hotel Murders
A Forensic Crime Scene Inquiry Lab

K.J. Sukhu

Victim 7
Description: No signs of foul play.
Gender: Male
Identity: Unknown

The Dolphin Hotel Murders
A Forensic Crime Scene Inquiry Lab

K.J. Sukhu

Character Profiles List
The following characters are the inhabitants of Floor 14 in the Dolphin Hotel

Here are the character profiles of the occupants of Floor 14 since the disaster. Figure out who the murderer(s) is/are and their victims.

Nikolai Astafurov (Age: 46)   Room 1445
Nikolai is the Russian ambassador. He was brought up with the ideals of communism but embraced the ideals of democracy. He was voted into office at an early age, and was thought to be a real contender to become a high ranking member of the Russian government. However, a political scandal halted his career temporarily when it came out that several politicians had been involved in severely mismanaging public funds. Nikolai was believed to have participated in this mismanagement but there was not enough evidence to convict him. To keep him out of the public eye and preserve his career, the government gave him the position of Ambassador to Persidia. He has slowly worked his way up to the position he currently holds. He has enjoyed his career but always felt like he squandered the chance to become a leader in his political party.

Kim Ye Park (Age: 41)   Room 1406
Kim is the North Korean ambassador. North Korea is a closed country. Normally politicians don't attend climate conferences; however, since the power change in North Korea, there has been an increase in the number of attendants. Kim is a fierce believer in communism and greatly opposes "free speech". He believes that under great leadership society can achieve more as a collective, rather than as a society where everyone looks out for themselves. Hypocritically Kim Ye Park is the son of Kim Ye Il who was a high ranking politician in North Korea. Kim Ye Park has always enjoyed privileged benefits while growing up in North Korea.

Ghobad Farshad (Age: 52)   Room 1426
Ghobad was once very opposed to the current Iranian administration. For a long time he advocated diplomacy with the Western world. He gained support from outside sources, but was persecuted at home. Eventually he was exiled from Iran at the age of 36. He found refuge in the international community and became a symbol of hope in the Middle East. The youth of Iran protested for his return for many years to no avail. Then in a surprising move by the Iranian government, the ban was lifted and he was asked to return home. The political move was surprising. Upon returning home, Ghobad was appointed as a special ambassador to the West. He has served in the post for three years.

Loyan Sheik (Age: 44)   Room ____
Loyan is a Somalian who has a profitable accounting business. Growing up in Somalia is tough, especially in Bosaso, an area known for high rates of extreme poverty. Food was scarce; his

shelter consisted of what would be considered a tent. He had several brothers and sisters whom he cared for. Obtaining an education was extremely difficult. It was normal for Loyan to walk several hours a day just to get to and from school. There weren't any gangs that caused him problems but there were warlords who controlled different territories. Warlords upheld their own "idealistic religious rules", which were mostly oppressive to the people. He spent the first twenty years of his life solely in Bosaso. He taught himself English and Math. When he was old enough he became somewhat of an activist, speaking up against the government in Somalia. A few people took notice and helped him advance his education. He achieved a degree in accounting and established his own accounting practice.

Raza Jehanzib (Age: 41)   Room 1443
Raza was from the city of Lahore, a place known for extremes. Half the population is wealthy and half the population is extremely poor. Raza was one of the lucky ones. Although he was born into wealth he never took it for granted. He tried to "make it" on his own by creating several businesses. However, he failed at every attempt. He always knew that if he hadn't been born into wealth that he might have been living on the street like so many others. Because of this he has tried to help organizations that aid the homeless. He wanted to be more helpful, but was too timid to assume a more responsible role.

Thien Vo Duong (Age: 32)   Room 1424
Thien came to the Dolphin all the way from Vietnam. She had always wanted to come to Izalith. At first she filed for a travel visa but secretly planned to stay as an illegal immigrant. She was about to go through with her plan until she met a man named Alfred Gomez. Alfred promised to take her out of Nha Trang and give her a charmed life in New Londo. The problem was that she was already married to a man named Trong Bao Duong. Thien wanted nothing more than to leave her fishing town and her old life behind her. So she ended up divorcing Trong and marrying Alfred. After a few days of marriage, she poisoned Alfred, withdrew all of his money from his bank account and tried to flee to Izalith on her own. Unfortunately, Trong stopped her before she could leave, physically beat her up for leaving him and threw acid on her. When the police showed up she claimed that Trong had killed Alfred and tried to kill her as well. Trong was arrested, and Thien got a huge payout on Alfred's life insurance. She came to Izalith to live the privileged life.

Thishanth Senmugalingam (Age: 26)   Room 1431
Thishanth grew up in Sri Lanka. He was born in the region of Badulla. However, that area was a very dangerous place for a Tamil to grow up in. The threat of being beaten by various Singhalese groups, or forced into military service by the Tamil Tigers was always real. He loved his Tamil and Singhalese neighbors and wished for the fighting to end. Eventually the risk became too much and he was forced to move to Jaffna. This region of Sri Lanka provided more of a safe haven for Tamils. But, after witnessing one of his best friends being forced to join the Tamil

The Dolphin Hotel Murders
A Forensic Crime Scene Inquiry Lab

K.J. Sukhu

Tigers, it too became apparent that even this town could not provide him with the security he desired. He filed for refugee status and applied for a receptionist position at the Dolphin Hotel.

Wright Walker (Age: 26)   Room ____

Wright is a Junior Manager at the Dolphin Hotel. He was a recent college graduate from the hospitality and tourism program at Izalith University. He finished with a very high G.P.A and was offered a position straight after University (which was rare for a hotel with a reputation like the Dolphin). His appointment wasn't smooth. In a short period of time he ruffled a few feathers. Many of the Senior Managers were annoyed with the ideas and changes he wanted to implement. He was known to favor some employees more than others and he routinely disregarded advice.

William Fraiser (Age: 41)   Room 1416

William is a father of four and a lawyer. He is a regular customer of the Dolphin Hotel. In fact, he frequently checked in specifically to the 14th floor because the Dolphin offered a lower rate due to the lower occupancy (otherwise he wouldn't normally be able to afford it). He worked in the town of Drewersville and drove up to the big city on the first Monday of every month. People say that the stress from being away from his family has weighed on him; others say that he has embraced his new role fully.

Nemo Renee (Age: 27)   Room 1428

Nemo is a technician who worked as an apprentice at the Dolphin. He always had a passion for fixing things and was very good at it. He hoped to go to school for engineering but didn't quite have the grades. Instead, he decided to become an apprentice in hopes of learning how things worked before opening up his own business.

Emily Jones (Age: 29)   Room 1400

Emily worked as an actuary for a very large consulting firm. Her job was to analyze data to figure out what rates insurance companies could charge to stay competitive while making high profits. Her job was very lucrative and had her travelling all over the world. She decided to go to Izalith on a whim to check out the shopping. When she arrived at the Dolphin the only vacancy was on the 14th floor. She was already checked into the hotel a few days before the storm hit. Her analytical skills are second to none.

Nick James Von Reimsdike (Age: 31)   Room ____

Nick is a 6'8, Dutch cyclist who was travelling to celebrate the "end of his single life". He came to Izalith with a friend to "party it up". When the trip was over he was supposed to get married back in the Netherlands. Nick has been on the professional cycling circuit for a few years. He's

The Dolphin Hotel Murders
A Forensic Crime Scene Inquiry Lab

K.J. Sukhu

an amazing athlete but has yet to win or come close to winning a race. He has mostly played a supporting role for the better members of his cycling team. A few years earlier he tried out for the Dutch Olympic team but was cut. He has since considered retiring from the cycling circuit to focus his attention on becoming a coach.

Ash Pikmin (Age: 29)   Room 1421
Ash is a bit of an odd person. He is a media student who is taking a semester off. In fact he has taken three semesters off in a row. He lives at home with his mother. However, hotel records show that he has checked into the Dolphin for at least one night every month. On his "Link'din" profile it states that he really enjoys media and media studies. He has a blog that he started a year ago that only contains two movie reviews and hasn't been updated since.

Dr. Lee (Age: 49)   Room 1411
Dr. Lee wasn't checked into the Dolphin. Instead, he was part of a team that was responding to a call on the 15th floor about the time the storm hit. A woman was giving birth in her hotel room. Complications arose and she couldn't make it to the hospital. When Dr. Lee arrived the situation had escalated to the point where both the baby and mother were in jeopardy of losing their lives. Just before they were about to start surgery, the power went out. The doctor and paramedics moved her to the 14th floor on the advice of the manager who informed them about the backup generators. They moved her and all of the equipment, but unfortunately there was little they could do. They ended up evacuating her to the hospital. During the commotion Dr. Lee had left his wallet in the hotel which the manager later found. Dr. Lee came back after his shift to retrieve his wallet. By that time the storm worsened, and there was no leaving after that.

Nicholas Brenner (Age: 19)   Room 1429
Nicholas is a very suspicious person. One day he just kind of showed up. When people ask him questions he displays a menacing smile. He talks to himself quite a bit. He has been seen arguing with himself and when you confront him he quiets down and smiles. He's 6'4 and built so people tend to leave him alone. In fact, mention his name around Floor 14 and people get quiet very quickly.

Chevar Timothy Morrison (Age: 32)   Room ____
This is Chevar's first time leaving Jamaica. He works in construction and spent most of his life saving up to travel the world. Unfortunately, a bad break-up with his girlfriend led to a messy situation where much of his money was stolen. He managed to get a portion of it back, but it was a major setback to his plans. Since then, he has become extremely jaded and doesn't trust people. He decided that he would spend his money on one really nice vacation rather than travelling around the world in one shot. Unfortunately he started the trip in Izalith and, due to the storm, this is where he remains.

The Dolphin Hotel Murders
A Forensic Crime Scene Inquiry Lab

K.J. Sukhu

Zuzana Holubova (Age: 39)   Room ____

Zuzana came to Izalith to work at the Dolphin 12 years ago. Originally from the Czech Republic, Zuzana was a cleaner at a four star hotel in Prague. She was hired by the manager of the Dolphin in an attempt to keep wages low, but maintain high standards. She neither hates nor loves her job but sees it as a necessity. What she really hates is the thought of working for someone for the rest of her life. She would love a way to "get out" of her current lifestyle but knows the odds of that are virtually impossible.

Femi Imami Kato (Age: Unknown)   Room 1419

Femi was the first President and Dictator of Equatorial Taris. He served for approximately 11 years. Unfortunately for him, he was thrown out of office by his nephew Kwadwo Kofi Osei in a military coup to take control of the country. Kwadwo is still in charge to this day and is the longest serving dictator on the continent of Aldera. Upon his defeat it was widely reported by several news outlets that Femi and several members of his regime were tried and found guilty of carrying out genocide. They were subsequently sentenced and executed. However, there is a man claiming to be Femi with delegates surrounding him. If the reports are true, this would be the first time in over twenty years that someone can confirm his existence.

Nicholas Carter Bright III (Age: 45)   Room 1427

Nick is a career politician from the UK and a member of the Commoner Imperial Faction (CIF). The CIF is a right wing political group that many view as being a racist political faction. The CIF has come under fire for many of their unusual policies. Namely, if you are not Caucasian or Asian, they discourage you from actually joining their party, but they still insist that they welcome non-Whites and non-Asians to vote alongside them. They have also made waves by declaring that many Muslims should not be granted British citizenship and should be deported. They blame Britain's sluggish economy on the "wave of immigrants" taking "real" British jobs. Mr. Bright was on unofficial business at the Dolphin.

Kieren Flynn (Age: 42)   Room ____

Kieren is an Irish stock trader who traded hedge funds and mortgages. Simply put, he dealt in debt. He would sell high risk mortgages to other banks and make a commission on the units sold. Then he would bet against the mortgages and make a killing when the banks foreclosed on the property. He went from being a small time stock trader to a millionaire in a matter of months when the "housing bubble" burst in Ireland. Much like what happened in America, many Irish families were losing their homes because of the weak economy. Kieren still resides in Ireland but spends a large portion of his time abroad. He's a regular at the Dolphin, and when the storm hit, he was one of the first to move down to the 14th floor and occupy a room.

The Dolphin Hotel Murders
A Forensic Crime Scene Inquiry Lab

K.J. Sukhu

Jorgen Himmler (Age: 28)   Room ____

Jorgen was put on trial for murder at the age of 14. He was charged with killing his father, Jordan Himmler. Jordan was the leader of a Neo-Nazi group and was having a troubled relationship with his son. Jorgen, who had a history of violence, was expelled from several schools. He claims that his father was constantly getting on his case and beat him on several occasions. He forced Jorgen into "military training" and told him that he wasn't strong enough. During one of these military operations he accidentally shot his father. He was convicted and, while serving his sentence in juvenile jail, was treated with several medications. Even though he has served his time, he is still under probation and must see his parole officer and psychiatrist once every two weeks. Jorgen couldn't afford to be staying at the Dolphin.

Laurent Abasi (Age: 29)   Room ____

Laurent is the supposed son of Ibada Abasi. Officially from the country of Kai, he left in 2000. Since leaving he has lived an ostentatious life. He has not returned home since. It was widely believed that he had found a new home in Europe. It was unclear why he was at the Dolphin. Usually he travels with his family, but for whatever reason, this time he had checked into the Dolphin with two bodyguards.

Benny Heidmen (Age: 28)   Room 1410

A year ago Benny was diagnosed with AIDS. His immune system is severely compromised and doctors have tried every drug and drug cocktail to give him a fighting chance but to no avail. Against doctors' orders, Benny decided to travel and "live his best days out in style". His second stop on his journey was the Dolphin.

Rohit Mahajan (Age: 31)   Room 1437

Rohit is a doctor and researcher from New Delhi. He has recently left his position at Fain Hospital due to an ongoing scandal. Rohit was in charge of clinical drug trials for several pharmaceutical companies. The position was very lucrative. Companies paid Rohit to test their drugs on patients. If the tests proved successful, then the drugs may be approved for retail. The controversy revolves around the people on whom Rohit tested the drugs. To test for certain heart medicines, Rohit would travel to the slums of Bihar. He would promise people free medicine if they signed a contract which was written in English. Many people did not know what they were signing and were never told that the drugs were for a clinical trial and were not proven. Many people died of heart attacks. When the scandal hit, Rohit resigned and left. The situation is still unravelling in India.

Ivan Restrepo Gil (Age: 43)   Room ____

Ivan is a part owner of a very lucrative taxi business in Columbia. He came from humble beginnings in Buenos Aries. He used to sell fruit to people stuck in traffic. He made his profit when he capitalized on a new rule that was being implemented in Columbia to reduce traffic. Residents would be issued special license plates. The ending of the license plates would dictate on what days people would be able to drive their cars. The only exception would be taxis and buses. He quickly applied for a special taxi license and started his own taxi service. It soon grew into a fleet. He quickly made a small fortune and now calls Envigado home. No one knows how he got the initial money to start up his business, but it seems to be a moot point now.

Hyeon Gi-Dong (Age: 54)   Room 1415
Hyeon Gi-Dong is a prominent stem cell researcher. Hyeon claimed that his team had produced a human embryo through cloning and had recovered stem cells from it. The team later claimed that they were close to being able to produce almost any embryo, no matter the organism. This news was celebrated with great hope, but those achievements were alleged to have been faked. Unfortunately his experiments were not easily reproducible and so, Hyeon, disgraced, left his native South Korea to shy away from negative attention. Hyeon has since moved his research team to the mountainous country of Tao. He still receives generous funding from an unknown source but his reputation has seen better days.

Constantine Ghibarivinova (Age: 47)   Room 1403
Officially Constantine is a member of the United Russian Political Party and aide to the ambassador. Constantine has been linked to several civil wars that have arisen in Aldera, South America and Eastern Europe. It is believed that he is an opportunistic weapons dealer. It cannot be confirmed how true this data is but it has been widely speculated.

Anthony Emmerson (Age: 41)   Room 1409
Anthony is a well-known lobbyist whose clients have included Quad Appeal, Xenoware Inc. and Infinitysoft. It is unclear as to the purpose of his stay at the Dolphin. Was it business or pleasure?

Jamie Emmerson (Age: 38)   Room 1409
Jamie runs a separate lobbying business from her husband and has clients such as Fickle, Presidium Green, Stasis Tech and Air Switch. She checked in with her husband, but no children.

Aa'idah Jiyad (Age: 29)   Room ____
Aa'idah is a prominent architect. She left Dubai to go to school in the West. She thought she would hate living in the Western world but actually fell in love with it. She attended school for architecture and finished at the top of her class. She was quickly recruited by an architectural firm based in Dubai and her first assignment was as a junior schematics surveyor on the Burj Khalifa.

The Dolphin Hotel Murders
A Forensic Crime Scene Inquiry Lab

K.J. Sukhu

Maeva Xavier (Age: 32)   Room ____

Maeva is a suspected terrorist and has several extradition orders against her. However, there is no such order in place in New Londo. She is closely watched, and there are several groups that want her extradited back to France to answer to a suspected bombing that killed two and injured one. There is no way that she could afford the Dolphin. It is believed that she must have been one of the people to take refuge in the Dolphin when the storm hit.

Robin Campelli (Age: 31)   Room 1423

Robin is a successful arbitrator. Her firm has made millions in settling disputes between companies and organizations. She's known for her cool, level headed style. She is a great listener and pretty good judge of character. Reportedly, she checked into the hotel for business related reasons.

April McEwan (Age: 29)   Room ____

April is a freelance reporter. She has contributed to major publications such as the Izalith Times and New Londo Today. She mostly covers political scandals. Her first big story was uncovering the affair between Senator Jason Barret and one of his secretaries. Since then she has reported on several affairs of prominent officials. She is adored by media outlets and hated by politicians and most of the private sector. For someone so young to be the one to uncover all of these scandals is remarkable. Where or how she gets her information remains unknown.

Adol Vice (Age: 42)   Room ____

Adol is an Austrian monk. He recently moved to the town of Drewersville to work at the church as part of a missionary exchange. He has a thick Austrian accent and is very reclusive. He is an eccentric man who seems to believe that most people are sinners. Because of his extremist views, many people seem to think that he may be on to something. He has attracted a cult following during the storm. He came to Izalith to make a fresh start after being accused of murder in Drewersville.

Andrew Isaha Makai (Age: 47)   Room 1413

Andrew is an Israeli recruiter. He is paid by his government to try and entice people with Israeli family history to move back to Israel in order to populate certain regions. He mostly targets middle to high income earners. As such, the government often has him checking into quite posh establishments. It's not strange to see him at the Dolphin, but it is unclear if he was there for business or pleasure.

The Dolphin Hotel Murders
A Forensic Crime Scene Inquiry Lab

K.J. Sukhu

Brigham Mosiah (Age: 23)   Room ____

Brigham once lived in an Amish community. At the age of 19 he was allowed to leave in order to experience the world to see if he could resist the temptations of sin. When he was exposed to newfound freedom, he went overboard. He partied, stole, lied and participated in unspecified crimes. It is believed that he has been charged with something major, but no information is available to the public. Needless to say he was disowned by his Amish community. To this day he says he would never go back to his small town, but admits he misses his family very much.

Jeff Chase (Age: 57)   Room 1433

Jeff is a convicted criminal. He was sentenced to jail for fifteen years after he was caught running an elaborate pyramid scheme. Jeff, who was a financial advisor, started his own company. He mostly preyed on ignorant clients who wanted to make money in the stock market. He would take a large sum of cash from his clients. Half of the money he took in, he would immediately pocket; the other half he would redistribute to clients to make it seem like the investments were paying off. He would then encourage them to put in more and get their friends to sign up. The plan worked well for years until his client base started to grow rapidly. Because of the size of his business, an audit by an independent company took place to see where his company ranked against other investment firms. At that point it was discovered that he had set up a ponsi scheme.

Emit Purel (Age: 59)   Room 1417

Emit is a long time lobbyist for several major private businesses. He gained notoriety however, with his work with Sigmaflow-Mart. Emit is known in many Southern and Western states for weakening the position of unions. He was the mind behind closing Sigmaflow-Mart stores if a union was about to take shape. He travels throughout the land, preaching that unions actually slow growth and do not allow for maximum productivity which will eventually lead to higher wages. His critics scoff at him because, by destroying unions many workers work for minimum wage, do not have a health care plan, work long hours and can get fired at any moment without an explanation.

Karel Novak (Age: 42)   Room 1405

Karel is a world renowned "Dungeon and Drakes" Dungeon Master. He travels to all the major tournaments and is famous for his imaginative realms and crazy twists that he throws at people. He was staying at the Dolphin while attending an event, so when the storm hit he was stuck in the Dolphin. Karel is described as a cocky, know-it-all who does not come by friends easily. Apparently he has already annoyed a lot of people.

The Dolphin Hotel Murders   K.J. Sukhu
A Forensic Crime Scene Inquiry Lab

Kale Anderson (Age: 56)   Room 1422

Mr. Anderson has been in the hospitality industry for quite some time. He started his career as a high school teacher. He taught a food and tourism class for several years until he opened up his own business, "Rent-me-Maid-to-Clean". The business took off rapidly but crashed just as quickly, leaving him unemployed. He then found work teaching again, this time at a community college. He stayed there for a few years until he accepted a junior management position at the prestigious All Seasons Hotel. He worked his way up the ladder until he became a Senior Manager in charge of all night shifts. At this point he transferred to the Dolphin when he was offered a similar position with a salary increase. He has been at the Dolphin ever since.

Dr. Aster Greendale (Age: 38)   Room 1441

Dr. Greendale is a general practitioner who recently lost his medical license. He has been implicated in a doping scandal. It seems that he would provide "performance enhancing drugs" to athletes at the professional level. He has also been accused of providing prescriptions to patients despite any real base of need. Currently, he has appealed the decision and is waiting for the appeal process to take place. Aster claims that he provided the anabolic drugs only to help heal damaged muscle and tissue sustained by the athletes and that he never personally injected the athletes.

The Dolphin Hotel Murders
A Forensic Crime Scene Inquiry Lab

K.J. Sukhu

Geographical Landscape
The Dolphin Hotel has changed since the storm hit

Here is a description of the floor plan for the 14th floor. It is important to note that more information on the landscape can be found throughout the entire case study package.

The Dolphin Hotel is composed of three distinct spires that merge into a "palm". The North Western spire is the longest. The central spire is a little more truncated and the North-Eastern spire is the shortest. Each hotel floor is equipped with almost everything a guest would require without needing to leave the floor. At the top of the central spire there is a Theatre for Performing Arts. In the "palm" of the floor layout is an Atrium. In fact the ceiling just above the Atrium of every floor contains glass that lets light beam down all the way to the bottom floor. Connected to the Atrium and directly West of it are two dining rooms; Dining Room B and Dining Room C. On the East side of the Atrium there is Dining Room A and Dining Room D. On any given night, each dining room offers food from a different region. To the very South of the floor's layout is a spa, library, and tea room. The guest rooms that run along the shortest spire to the South of the floor are all decorated in a classic style. The rooms located in the centre of the floor are decorated in a contemporary style. Lastly, the rooms starting from the North-Western spire running to the South of the hotel are decorated in a classic-cottage hybrid style.

The Dolphin Hotel Murders
A Forensic Crime Scene Inquiry Lab

K.J. Sukhu

Interviews With Residents
The following statements were given by residents of the Dolphin Hotel

Here is an account of various statements gathered around the hotel. The information that is being relayed to you is not time stamped. Meaning, that some statements could be weeks or months old and some could have just recently been taken.

Note: *Some reports may be true and some may be false*
People can say what they want but remember some people lie and some people speak the truth. Some people's truth may also be distorted, but you have the power of scientific discovery on your side.

Thien — "Things are a mess outside. People are always complaining about the amount of food they get but I'm grateful to our leader. Everyone is fed, there's order and safety. If people don't like what's going on they should think about leaving."

Zuzana — "I've been saved. I lived a life that shouldn't have belonged to me. I see that now. I live right. This symbol is a sign to honor the One who gave me the insight I needed."

Unknown — "You know this place is run by a bunch of crooked people, but I think the constant preaching is the worst thing about it. Everything in here is so tightly controlled. Why has he been allowed to go and talk wherever and about whatever he wants?"

Ivan — "Order #59: All residents must stay confined to their rooms unless permission has been granted. Failure to do so will result in a loss of food privileges or a meeting with Miss. Jones."

Wright — "Freedom fighters? You gotta be kidding me! No. A so called 'freedom fighter' is nothing more than a terrorist. If you talk to their group they'll say the opposite, that 'terrorists are someone's freedom fighters'. But we should be helping one another not fighting one another and putting all we have at risk."

Jeff — "Huh? Oh. When Bill needs me he calls me to a conference room. I've never actually seen the inside of the room. He puts the food in the hallway before he summons me. He hands me a list of rooms to distribute the food to and I do it. It's definitely not a bad job. There are a lot worse you can get here."

The Dolphin Hotel Murders
A Forensic Crime Scene Inquiry Lab

K.J. Sukhu

Medical Log	????? – treated for physical bruises and bone fractures – wooden splint put on left arm and leg. ????? – ??? Karel – treated for physical bruises and malnutrition - ???????????????????????? Raza – treated for severe malnutrition - ???????????????????????????????????????
Raza	"Emily usually gives either a light one or a heavy one. For a heavy one you're going to find yourself in the 'care' of either Chevar or Nicholas. And a light one is several nights in the atrium with no blanket or anything. Personally, hypothermia is more inviting than the alternative."
Unknown	"There is a distinct difference in the behavior of the doctors at the beginning of the storm and now. Very distinct."
Kieren	"Everyone knows that Benny has AIDS. He's been seeing the doctors regularly. Honestly I don't think he should be staying with us. Do you know how contagious that disease is? Anyhow, no one can say anything without 'what's her face' going crazy."
Unknown	"The manager controls everything. He controls the food distribution, jobs shifts, everything... but he's doing a good job. No one would have survived without him."
Robin	"This is a corrupt place, and don't let anyone tell you any different. Some people are above the law. Why are they above the law? Because of their 'special talents'. These people prey on the weak. I've never been a real advocate before, but this situation has definitely made me think a little differently."
Unknown	"I think I got sick a few months back, sometime after the 'special harvest'."
April	"People have always wanted to know where I get my information, but I don't think they'll ever find out. In fact, now I'm pretty confident no one will find out."
Unknown	"I would never complain about food. I know some people did and shortly after they changed... they weren't beat up physically or anything, they just changed... you know?"
Unknown	"You take what you can. Some days food is given out, other days you have to go hungry. Basically, if Bill presents you with food you have two choices, eat or starve."

The Dolphin Hotel Murders
A Forensic Crime Scene Inquiry Lab

K.J. Sukhu

Unknown	"There's been an illness outbreak in the last few months. I think that's why there's been a sort of quarantine set up. The strange thing is though that the doctors don't seem at all concerned by it. They interact with the sick just as they would with the 'healthy'. It's kind of strange."
Unknown	"I'm not sure why Emily hasn't ordered down the pictures of that weird Swiss flower posted in front of rooms 1420, 1435, and 1438. It may seem like people are trying to add some cheer to the floor, but it seems a little off to me."
Femi	"Reimsdike has a few men who work for him as his 'security team'. Of course they had to be approved by 'you know who'. Anyway they recently instituted random spot checks and a curfew. When night is upon us, the doors are locked together from the outside so no one can leave their room."
Unknown	"Unbelievably, the sick are being treated by the doctors. Not just 'check ups' but they actually get medicine. How this is possible is beyond me but kudos to those doctors. I have no idea how that's even remotely possible."
Ghobad	"People don't want to believe that there is a hierarchy, but there is. Look at Pikmin and some others, I'd guess that that kid has actually gained weight."
Unknown	"He uses a few people as his 'security' to make sure no one ever tries to steal food or resources. He instituted it after a struggle that occurred. I'm sure you're going to figure all the politics out."
Aa'idah	"Walker is good. The doctors are good. They take care of me."
Nicholas	"Kim and Nikolai both have big mouths. Too bad no one can understand them."
Dr. Lee	"Yes, there was a body rotting in… Conference Room D, I believe. You should confirm that with Nick. He found the body. Anyhow, what I can tell you is that it was there for a while because rotting had set in. I'm surprised no one noticed it earlier with the smell. The body had some stab marks in the back. There was nothing really unusual other than the fact that most of the pockets were turned inside out, yet there was a bottle of water and a candy bar found beside the corpse. Both of which are extremely valuable in a society like this."
Laurent	"I got the order from Riemsdike to put Anthony and Jamie in the care of our two 'caretakers', simply because I suppose their relationship was a bit of a concern to the higher ups."

The Dolphin Hotel Murders
A Forensic Crime Scene Inquiry Lab

K.J. Sukhu

Unknown	"I wish those 'freedom fighters' would have never tried what they did. After that mess security got much tighter, and no one is better off for it."
Karel	"I don't know what's going on. I'm here because I deserve it. Please tell Emily to reconsider her stance. But please don't say anything to Chevar or Nicholas. Please. I'll do anything. I thought waking up every morning, listening to the preaching of the end of the world through the wall was bad, but that would be paradise now."
From the Desk of Dr. Rohit Mahajan	I believe I have finalized the formula based on the available chemicals on hand. Regrettably I won't know the potency of the drug until the pills are actually created. However, this remains an exciting prospect. Based on the first experiment with drug 'A', the higher ups seem very enthusiastic about our expertise. I too must admit that I was surprised that our young friend was able to create the compound based on the formula provided.
Kale	"I suppose it was controversial at the time, but it helped reassure the customers. If you have all employees' DNA on file, then no one would dare steal anything, right? Well anyhow, a law came into effect stating that you can't do that so I guess it's a moot point now."
Jeff	"My arrangement has worked out nicely. I have created an ongoing distraction and in return my life is peaceful and… predictable. I'll weather this storm out and leave unscathed with a clear conscience. I just need to figure out how to shut that born again guy up. I can hear him through the walls every day. It's actually kind of ironic when you think about it."
A Note Scribbled on a Paper	We've calculated that 70% of food stock remains. Other than the 'Four' and the so called 'King', all residents have consumed 4 % of the entire stock. Our leaders have by themselves consumed 3%. If you want to see a change then consider joining us.
Nick:	"This place is totally safe. Anyone who tried to rebel has been punished in one way or another. It has become a sign to all residents and has solidified our leader's rule. Life is finally 'normal'."
Unknown:	"In the beginning, Jeff used to go to room 1420 all the time. Recently, though, I haven't seen him come around."
Dr. Aster's Personal Log	It would seem that as the days go by we have become more important, as has our chemist friend. It would be beneficial to see how much our friend is being paid for his contribution. I can see a power shift occurring soon with many potential benefits on the horizons.

The Dolphin Hotel Murders
A Forensic Crime Scene Inquiry Lab

K.J. Sukhu

Audio Message of Kieren	"Listen, why can't we be on top? We're smarter than the whole lot of these guys. We might not be able to touch the 'King', but we would be able to get to one of the horsemen."
Ivan	"Order #13: All those who refuse food forfeit their right to future meals. Food is not a right, it's a privilege."
Unknown	"If Andrew or Laurent come to get you, you stand a chance and get to go to room 1430 to explain your situation. If Riemsdike comes, then your fate may already be sealed."
Constantine	"If you were in my position you would have done it too. I needed a safety net. Do you know how unnerving it is to sleep next door to a psychopath? Let's see you live like how I was living and see if you would have done things differently."
Brigham	"This whole experience has really opened my eyes to who and what I've become. I realize the error of my ways and I will heed the advice given to me and do away with sin. I am ashamed of who I was."
Unknown	"I think the 'freedom fighters' might have succeeded had they selected better potential members. They seemed to have been gaining traction and then all of a sudden, boom! They must have reached out to the wrong person."
Nicholas	"This world is more real to me than any previous version. I feel at home, I feel alive."
Adol Vice	"Everywhere I go there is controversy. Some say that I am the root of the cause, but an observant man would see that I am an instrument of chaos sent to cleanse the land of wickedness and sin. None here are clean and so I was delivered. I have no use for any structure or worldly power. All I know is the Word."
Unknown	Person 1: "What do you want to do with him?" Person 2: "I'm not sure. He's served me well but I need him to know who runs the show, and that he can't make moves without me." Person 1: "This is a tough position… maybe we could let this go and just talk to him?" Person 2: "How do you talk to a person like that?" Person 1: "To be honest, I don't even like being in the same room as him…" Person 2: "Yeah… I'll deal with him. Go bring him to me… but go alone and don't bring anyone with you."

IMPORTANT: This report contains proprietary and original material. Accordingly, this document may not be copied or released to third parties without consent.

The Dolphin Hotel Murders   K.J. Sukhu
A Forensic Crime Scene Inquiry Lab

Note from Constantine	Please be advised that two individuals who are close (even before they checked into the Dolphin) are plotting against one of the 'Four'. I have overheard statements and plans to usurp one of their positions to make life more favorable. I trust you know of whom I speak. I write this at great risk to myself in order to better communication between myself and our great leadership.
Unknown	"Nick has got almost the exact same room as Emily, so right there that should tell you something."
Unknown	"The occupant of room 1402 gets special treatment. It's no secret. You can tell by the couple that was thrown in jail that there are a lot of advantages to being friends with 'higher ups'. How do I know they're friends? I've seen the person visit the theatre."
Unknown	"Jorgen's a tool. All he does is sit and listen to that fool preach. If that's how he wants to spend his time, that's fine. I'd rather devise a way to take more control of my life."
Nicholas	"My brother, Chevar? He and I are the same and… different. While I like his results, I don't agree with his approach. He definitely works well by himself but I think he appreciates working with a group. Me, I couldn't stand it. And those others are horrible to work with. Since that day I knew that I would only take on a task that's solo. I just think anything else isn't as elegant."
Thishanth	"My life will never be the same. I'm a different person than when I came in here. If others survive they can heal. I've been in a bad place before, but this… this is different, how could this have happened? It's almost impossible. This doesn't make any sense."
Unknown	"I haven't seen Loyan for a while. But he lives across from Ivan. Yeah I know he's got a pretty nice place."
Unknown	"It's no secret that William had a thing for Maeva, so there's no surprise his room is next to hers. Too bad he gets shot down repeatedly. She's a strong woman."
Unknown	"Yeah, they put some of the 'zombies' near the tall spire. The girl in room 1425 is oblivious to anything and I think the same goes for the guy in room 1412. It's either that or he's a huge jerk."
Benny	"I trusted Dr. Lee, but he sold me out to Hyeon."

The Dolphin Hotel Murders
A Forensic Crime Scene Inquiry Lab

K.J. Sukhu

Recorded Conversation	Unknown Male:	"Are you sure about this?"
	Unknown Female:	"It came from the top."
	Unknown Male:	"Yeah, but he's one of us."
	Unknown Female:	"He's been getting more and more unstable and violent, look what he's been doing to …"
	Unknown Male:	"What am I supposed to do with him?"
	Unknown Female:	"We're supposed to take him to the theatre room and from there; we're all going to make a decision about him going forward."

Constantine "Femi has been a life saver. A small piece of food is a small price to pay for a small treat. It's funny too, anyone who knows me from the outside would not think of me as wanting it, but here, it's definitely handy."

Robin "I woke up and he was gone. I don't remember… I don't remember. I was better before that. I'm not ok. Where did he go? Where did they take him?"

Unknown "It's unusual to think that before the storm, the dining rooms were a place of food and delight, and now they're the center of starvation and dread. What a crazy situation!"

Audio Recording	Person 1:	"Why did you have to do this?"
	Person 2:	"It was for your own good. You were becoming…dependent."
	Person 1:	"Why didn't you come and tell me before [*sobbing*]?"
	Person 2:	"As I said, it was for your own good [*pause*]. Listen; is this going to be a problem going forward?"
	Person 1:	[*sobbing*] "No. [*sniff*] I'll do my job."
	Person 2:	"Good, I count on you."
	Person 1:	[*sniff*] "Thanks."
	Person 2:	"And hey, don't blame him, he was just following orders."

Unknown "Be warned. There is still unholy actions amongst these residents. Many drink to the point of intoxication; a deadly sin that I have warned them about many times. The 'higher ups' get drunk off of wine and the 'others' get drunk on hooch."

Unknown "The southern rooms of the atrium were set up after the 'attempt'. At that point, Chevar, Nicholas and Emily were granted their positions."

IMPORTANT: This report contains proprietary and original material. Accordingly, this document may not be copied or released to third parties without consent.

The Dolphin Hotel Murders
A Forensic Crime Scene Inquiry Lab

K.J. Sukhu

Kim Ye	"경호원 둘이 나를 학대했어요.그들은 나를 침묵시킬수는 없어요. 나는 자마이칸애들이나 다른사람들을 두려워하지 않아요. 그들은 지금 조그만 권력을 즐겨하지만 이런사람들은 이 담밖에서는 아무것도 못하지요.내가 여기서 말하고 싶고 하고싶은 것은 더 강력한 해결책입니다. 그래서 이폭풍이 빨리 끝나서 새로운 시절이 시작되는겁니다."
Unknown	"I've heard and smelled strange things coming from room 1408. On more than one occasion I even thought I heard a loud bang. I'm not gonna speculate about what went on in there. It's funny because I don't even know if anyone is assigned to that room."
Chevar Timothy Morrison	"Wukinn' for de 'King' is great. Me a get great food, me do wat me like, and I be in charge of all des people. I don't owe dem nuthin. Me know it would nevah wuk so me a go to de 'King'. 'im ask me to do 'im a solid and look how I be rewarded. Dem just bandulu."
Unknown	"Ghobad? … Yeah that guy was a great guy. But big risk, big reward. Life would have been different for us all… but you can't live with 'what ifs'."
Unknown	"People think being in a higher position is easy. Believe me, it's hard; I've had to do things I regret just to keep the peace. I've taken orders and have given orders that I will almost always regret. But because of my strength I was tasked with that role."
Andrew	"It's no one's business where I got this scar on my cheek. But it pisses me off every time I have to look at it. It's also a reminder of what happened here. I have to survive here. What's the expression? 'It's a dog – eat – dog world'."
Unknown	"No one ever really goes into Conference Room C. I think they store a lot of supplies in there. Well… it's just a guess because I saw Laurent once going in there with some rope and I know Nemo sometimes stores a ladder in there so that would be my best guess."
Unknown	"Chevar and Nickolas? I don't know who's worse. One's a raging psychopath and the other is a quiet psychopath. I'm just glad Emily showed mercy on me. I realize now that my old way of thinking was wrong."

The Dolphin Hotel Murders
A Forensic Crime Scene Inquiry Lab

K.J. Sukhu

Thishanth	"Nemo installed several clamps on all the generators. So if you want to take a look at them you're going to have to talk to him or the 'King'. Some people say that it's meant as a safety device but it's an obvious attempt to control the power."
Nikolai	"What is it that you want? You have to think about life after here. You have to think about the future. I've got money. I can make it so that you never have to work again. Pick a country, I can set you up there for life. Just please, I need food and water. Скажи мне… Дай мне ответ. Я клянусь, если я когда-нибудь выберусь отсюда я заставлю тебя и всех здесь присутствующих пожалеть об этом!"
Unknown	"It's much quieter now. Much quieter."
Unknown	"I honestly think I'm so hungry I'm imagining things. About a month ago I could swear I smelled barbeque. It was divine, but it had to be my imagination… it just had to."
Unknown	"Emily's lap dog lives next to her 'office'. I guess she wants to keep her pet close on hand."

The Dolphin Hotel Murders
A Forensic Crime Scene Inquiry Lab

K.J. Sukhu

Statements Taken From Associates Outside the Dolphin

Information has been gathered for you from people connected to the people involved in the investigation

This may or may not help with establishing relationships or explain why some people went to the Dolphin in the first place.

Statement from Barry and Delilah Arbitrators:
We are all hopeful for the safe return of Robin. It is however public knowledge that she left our firm two weeks before she left for Izalith. We actually had a messy 'break-up'. Our firm relied on her public relations skills, which allowed our arbitrators to work without distraction. However, we did wish her success with her new startup firm, we just disagreed on the timing.

Indian Authorities:
"The investigation is still ongoing. It doesn't matter where he's located right now. If he is found guilty he will be returned to India and he will stand for sentencing. Besides, we know where he is located and why he was there."

Audry Miles (British Politician):
"It's no secret my feelings towards Nick. I mean I don't agree with his beliefs, I am on record saying that I'm happy that his party lost seats in the last election. I even questioned his trip because I have it on good information that he went in order to secure large funds for his campaign. But I would never wish this on anyone…ever."

Iconic Theory Research Black Inc. Receptionist:
"The doctor left for Izalith for both business and personal matters. It's hard to get research grants in this part of the world due to …'you know what' but I believe he went to investigate opportunities in the West. I believe he also went to see what his reputation was like over there."

Identity Withheld:
"My foolhardy brother left to look into building some sort of poor people shelter… I told that idiot to just be thankful for what he has."

Austrian Ministries:
"After the fiasco in Drewersville, Adol and our church parted ways. We gave him a severance package and he agreed that he would stop preaching for us. He did say that he would preach his own gospel, the 'true' gospel. We're happy this situation is behind us. We continue to pray for him as well as the people he has tricked into following him."

Protected Identity (incarcerated male):
"I was his cell mate for five years. He hasn't changed. He told me he had a new arrangement all figured out. Some way where he gets off tax free and can get rich off donations. He just said he needed to meet the right character. I guess he found that character in Izalith."

Scythe Financial:
"Hopefully Emit can work his magic. The prospect of finally placing some products in that closed market is tantalizing."

Palestinian Activist:
"The recruiter went to secure weapons. He had a meeting with a well-known arms dealer. Why else would he be there? When will the world open up their eyes to what's going on?"

Newspaper Editor of Izalith times:
"You know, I still don't know where she gets her info but whenever she shows up with a story we don't even need to check a fact. That's how reliable her stories are. If I were a politician I would be very nice to her because she could ruin someone's career. But I still don't know where she gets her info. Who could have such personal info on so many different politicians from all over? In any case she hasn't contributed a story in a while, I guess she was getting some new info at Izalith."

Parole Officer:
"She can't go back to that life she once had. It may be fast money but it's dangerous. Luckily she has been clean for the last little while. But I'm really concerned with this guy she's been seeing. They email constantly and they apparently meet up regularly at the Dolphin. It's just not a healthy relationship."

Israeli Activist:
"The Israeli delegate went to talk to a member of the Russian Political Party to investigate a sale of weapons to several Middle Eastern countries. Don't let anyone else spin it differently."

The Dolphin Hotel Murders
A Forensic Crime Scene Inquiry Lab

K.J. Sukhu

Blood Analysis
Blood reports for all residents of Floor 14

Blood analysis taken from all residents (time of sample taken cannot be verified).

Note: Different regions of the world use different units for blood work. Units were chosen based on ease of research for students.

Person	Chemical Breakdown	
Nikolai Astafurov	Serum Albumin = 1.9 g/dL Saffron extract = positive Creatinine = 115 umol/L Glucose = N/A 3'- azido-3'-deoxythymidine = negative Creatine phosphokinase = 185 U/L	BAC = 0.00% Cocaine = 0.00mg/L THC = 0 ng/mL N-methyl-1-phenylpropan-2-amine = negative 7-AminoFlunitrazepam = positive
Kim Ye Park	Serum Albumin = 2.4 g/dL Saffron extract = positive Creatinine = 114 umol/L Glucose = N/A 3'- azido-3'-deoxythymidine = negative Creatine phosphokinase = 180 U/L	BAC = 0.00% Cocaine = 0.00mg/L THC = 0 ng/mL N-methyl-1-phenylpropan-2-amine = negative 7-AminoFlunitrazepam = positive
Ghobad Farshad	Serum Albumin = 3.0 g/dL Saffron extract = negative Creatinine = 98 umol/L Glucose = N/A 3'- azido-3'-deoxythymidine = positive Creatine phosphokinase = 69 U/L	BAC = 0.00% Cocaine = 0.00mg/L THC = 0 ng/mL N-methyl-1-phenylpropan-2-amine - negative 7-AminoFlunitrazepam = negative
Loyan Sheik	Serum Albumin = 3.8 g/dL Saffron extract = negative Creatinine = 115 umol/L Glucose = N/A 3'- azido-3'-deoxythymidine = negative Creatine phosphokinase = 98 U/L	BAC = 0.00% Cocaine = 0.00mg/L THC = 0 ng/mL N-methyl-1-phenylpropan-2-amine = negative 7-AminoFlunitrazepam = positive
Raza Jehanzib	Serum Albumin =2.7 g/dL Saffron extract = negative Creatinine = 95 umol/L Glucose = N/A 3'- azido-3'-deoxythymidine = negative Creatine phosphokinase = 178U/L	BAC = 0.00% Cocaine = 0.00mg/L THC = 0 ng/mL N-methyl-1-phenylpropan-2-amine = negative 7-AminoFlunitrazepam = positive
Thien Vo Duong	Serum Albumin = 3.4 g/dL Saffron extract = negative Creatinine = 60 umol/L Glucose = N/A 3'- azido-3'-deoxythymidine = negative Creatine phosphokinase = 135 U/L	BAC = 0.011% Cocaine = 0.00mg/L THC = 0 ng/mL N-methyl-1-phenylpropan-2-amine = negative 7-AminoFlunitrazepam = negative

IMPORTANT: This report contains proprietary and original material. Accordingly, this document may not be copied or released to third parties without consent.

The Dolphin Hotel Murders   K.J. Sukhu
A Forensic Crime Scene Inquiry Lab

Name	Panel 1	Panel 2
Thishanth Senmugalingam	Serum Albumin = 2.5 g/dL Saffron extract = negative Creatinine = 108 umol/L Glucose = N/A 3'- azido-3'-deoxythymidine = positive Creatine phosphokinase = 60 U/L	BAC = 0.00% Cocaine = 0.00mg/L THC = 0 ng/mL N-methyl-1-phenylpropan-2-amine = negative 7-AminoFlunitrazepam = positive
Wright Walker	Serum Albumin = 4.2 g/dL Saffron extract = negative Creatinine = 55 umol/L Glucose = N/A 3'- azido-3'-deoxythymidine = negative Creatine phosphokinase =72 U/L	BAC = 0.014% Cocaine = 0.01mg/L THC = 54 ng/mL N-methyl-1-phenylpropan-2-amine = negative 7-AminoFlunitrazepam = negative
William Fraiser	Serum Albumin = 3.7 g/dL Saffron extract = negative Creatinine = 55 umol/L Glucose = N/A 3'- azido-3'-deoxythymidine = negative Creatine phosphokinase = 64 U/L	BAC = 0.029% Cocaine = 0.00mg/L THC = 101 ng/mL N-methyl-1-phenylpropan-2-amine = negative 7-AminoFlunitrazepam = negative
Dr. Lee	Serum Albumin = 5.1g/dL Saffron extract = negative Creatinine = 45 umol/L Glucose = N/A 3'- azido-3'-deoxythymidine = negative Creatine phosphokinase = 95 U/L	BAC = 0.025% Cocaine = 0.00mg/L THC = 34 ng/mL N-methyl-1-phenylpropan-2-amine = negative 7-AminoFlunitrazepam = negative
Chevar Timothy Morrison	Serum Albumin = 3.5 g/dL Saffron extract = negative Creatinine = 65 umol/L Glucose = N/A 3'- azido-3'-deoxythymidine = negative Creatine phosphokinase = 123 U/L	BAC = 0.32% Cocaine = 0.00mg/L THC = 0 ng/mL N-methyl-1-phenylpropan-2-amine = positive 7-AminoFlunitrazepam = negative
Zuzana Holubova	Serum Albumin = 2.9 g/dL Saffron extract = negative Creatinine = 70 umol/L Glucose = N/A 3'- azido-3'-deoxythymidine = negative Creatine phosphokinase = 130 U/L	BAC = 0.00% Cocaine = 0.00mg/L THC = 0 ng/mL N-methyl-1-phenylpropan-2-amine = negative 7-AminoFlunitrazepam = negative
Nemo Renee	Serum Albumin = 4.2 g/dL Saffron extract = negative Creatinine = 69 umol/L Glucose – N/A 3'- azido-3'-deoxythymidine = negative Creatine phosphokinase = 99 U/L	BAC = 0.018% Cocaine = 0.00mg/L THC = 0.002 ng/mL N-methyl-1-phenylpropan-2-amine = negative 7-AminoFlunitrazepam = negative
Emily Jones	Serum Albumin = 3.9 g/dL Saffron extract = negative Creatinine = 55 umol/L Glucose = N/A 3'- azido-3'-deoxythymidine = negative Creatine phosphokinase = 111 U/L	BAC = 0.018% Cocaine = 0.00mg/L THC = 0.001 ng/mL N-methyl-1-phenylpropan-2-amine = negative 7-AminoFlunitrazepam = negative

The Dolphin Hotel Murders
A Forensic Crime Scene Inquiry Lab

K.J. Sukhu

Jorgen Himmler	Serum Albumin = 3.5 g/dL Saffron extract = negative Creatinine = 89 umol/L Glucose = N/A 3'- azido-3'-deoxythymidine = negative Creatine phosphokinase = 63 U/L	BAC = 0.00% Cocaine = 0.00mg/L THC = 0 ng/mL N-methyl-1-phenylpropan-2-amine = negative 7-AminoFlunitrazepam = negative
Kieren Flynn	Serum Albumin = 2.7 g/dL Saffron extract = negative Creatinine = 96 umol/L Glucose = N/A 3'- azido-3'-deoxythymidine = negative Creatine phosphokinase = 79 U/L	BAC = 0.09% Cocaine = 0.06mg/L THC = 135 ng/mL N-methyl-1-phenylpropan-2-amine = positive 7-AminoFlunitrazepam = positive
Laurent Abasi	Serum Albumin = 3.7 g/dL Saffron extract = negative Creatinine = 78 umol/L Glucose = N/A 3'- azido-3'-deoxythymidine = negative Creatine phosphokinase = 144 U/L	BAC = 0.028% Cocaine = 0.00mg/L THC = 0 ng/mL N-methyl-1-phenylpropan-2-amine = negative 7-AminoFlunitrazepam = negative
Benny Heidmen	Serum Albumin = 2.85 g/dL Saffron extract = negative Creatinine = 88 umol/L Glucose = N/A 3'- azido-3'-deoxythymidine = positive Creatine phosphokinase = 140 U/L	BAC = 0.00% Cocaine = 0.00mg/L THC = 0 ng/mL N-methyl-1-phenylpropan-2-amine = negative 7-AminoFlunitrazepam = positive
Nick James Von Reimsdike	Serum Albumin = 4.1 g/dL Saffron extract = negative Creatinine = 68 umol/L Glucose = N/A 3'- azido-3'-deoxythymidine = negative Creatine phosphokinase = 150 U/L	BAC = 0.029% Cocaine = 0.00mg/L THC = 0.31 ng/mL N-methyl-1-phenylpropan-2-amine = negative 7-AminoFlunitrazepam = negative
Ash Pikmin	Serum Albumin = 3.4 g/dL Saffron extract = negative Creatinine = 58 umol/L Glucose = N/A 3'- azido-3'-deoxythymidine = negative Creatine phosphokinase = 50 U/L	BAC = 0.032% Cocaine = 0.02mg/L THC = 112 ng/mL N-methyl-1-phenylpropan-2-amine = positive 7-AminoFlunitrazepam = negative
Femi Imami Kato	Serum Albumin = 1.8 g/dL Saffron extract = negative Creatinine = 108 umol/L Glucose = N/A 3'- azido-3'-deoxythymidine = negative Creatine phosphokinase = 98 U/L	BAC = 0.054% Cocaine = 0.00mg/L THC = 0 ng/mL N-methyl-1-phenylpropan-2-amine = negative 7-AminoFlunitrazepam = negative
Nicholas Carter Bright III	Serum Albumin = 2.9 g/dL Saffron extract = negative Creatinine = 78 umol/L Glucose = N/A 3'- azido-3'-deoxythymidine = negative Creatine phosphokinase = 98 U/L	BAC = 0.00% Cocaine = 0.00mg/L THC = 0 ng/mL N-methyl-1-phenylpropan-2-amine = positive 7-AminoFlunitrazepam = positive

The Dolphin Hotel Murders
A Forensic Crime Scene Inquiry Lab

K.J. Sukhu

Rohit Mahajan	Serum Albumin = 3.7 g/dL Saffron extract = negative Creatinine = 50 umol/L Glucose = N/A 3'- azido-3'-deoxythymidine = negative Creatine phosphokinase = 70 U/L	BAC = 0.010% Cocaine = 0.00mg/L THC = 0.32 ng/mL N-methyl-1-phenylpropan-2-amine = negative 7-AminoFlunitrazepam = negative
Ivan Restrepo Gil	Serum Albumin = 3.4 g/dL Saffron extract = negative Creatinine = 19 umol/L Glucose = N/A 3'- azido-3'-deoxythymidine = negative Creatine phosphokinase = 165 U/L	BAC = 0.010% Cocaine = 0.00mg/L THC = 0 ng/mL N-methyl-1-phenylpropan-2-amine = negative 7-AminoFlunitrazepam = negative
Anthony Emmerson	Serum Albumin = 2.5 g/dL Saffron extract = positive Creatinine = 98 umol/L Glucose = N/A 3'- azido-3'-deoxythymidine = negative Creatine phosphokinase = 185 U/L	BAC = 0.00% Cocaine = 0.00mg/L THC = 0 ng/mL N-methyl-1-phenylpropan-2-amine = negative 7-AminoFlunitrazepam = positive
Jamie Emmerson	Serum Albumin = 3.1 g/dL Saffron extract = positive Creatinine = 117 umol/L Glucose = N/A 3'- azido-3'-deoxythymidine = negative Creatine phosphokinase = 150 U/L	BAC = 0.00% Cocaine = 0.00mg/L THC = 0 ng/mL N-methyl-1-phenylpropan-2-amine = negative 7-AminoFlunitrazepam = negative
Maeva Xavier	Serum Albumin = 3.1 g/dL Saffron extract = negative Creatinine = 95 umol/L Glucose = N/A 3'- azido-3'-deoxythymidine = negative Creatine phosphokinase = 165U/L	BAC = 0.00% Cocaine = 0.00mg/L THC = 0 ng/mL N-methyl-1-phenylpropan-2-amine = negative 7-AminoFlunitrazepam = negative
Aa'idah Jiyad	Serum Albumin = 2.6 g/dL Saffron extract = negative Creatinine = 82 umol/L Glucose = N/A 3'- azido-3'-deoxythymidine = negative Creatine phosphokinase = 117 U/L	BAC = 0.00% Cocaine = 0.01mg/L THC = 0 ng/mL N-methyl-1-phenylpropan-2-amine = positive 7-AminoFlunitrazepam = positive
Robin Campelli	Serum Albumin = 3.4 g/dL Saffron extract = negative Creatinine = 79 umol/L Glucose = N/A 3'- azido-3'-deoxythymidine = negative Creatine phosphokinase = 123 U/L	BAC = 0.00% Cocaine = 0.00mg/L THC = 0 ng/mL N-methyl-1-phenylpropan-2-amine = positive 7-AminoFlunitrazepam = positive
April McEwan	Serum Albumin = 4.1 g/dL Saffron extract = negative Creatinine = 61 umol/L Glucose = N/A 3'- azido-3'-deoxythymidine = negative Creatine phosphokinase = 95 U/L	BAC = 0.031% Cocaine = 0.01mg/L THC = 0.31 ng/mL N-methyl-1-phenylpropan-2-amine = negative 7-AminoFlunitrazepam = negative

IMPORTANT: This report contains proprietary and original material. Accordingly, this document may not be copied or released to third parties without consent.

The Dolphin Hotel Murders
A Forensic Crime Scene Inquiry Lab

K.J. Sukhu

Adol Vice	Serum Albumin = 3.38 g/dL Saffron extract = negative Creatinine = 42 umol/L Glucose = N/A 3'- azido-3'-deoxythymidine = negative Creatine phosphokinase = 43 U/L	BAC = 0.00% Cocaine = 0.00mg/L THC = 0 ng/mL N-methyl-1-phenylpropan-2-amine = negative 7-AminoFlunitrazepam = negative
Andrew Isaha Makai	Serum Albumin = 4.1 g/dL Saffron extract = negative Creatinine = 59 umol/L Glucose = N/A 3'- azido-3'-deoxythymidine = negative Creatine phosphokinase = 53 U/L	BAC = 0.023% Cocaine = 0.00mg/L THC = 0.11 ng/mL N-methyl-1-phenylpropan-2-amine = negative 7-AminoFlunitrazepam = negative
Brigham Mosiah	Serum Albumin = 3.7 g/dL Saffron extract = negative Creatinine = 69 umol/L Glucose = N/A 3'- azido-3'-deoxythymidine = negative Creatine phosphokinase = 53 U/L	BAC = 0.00% Cocaine = 0.00mg/L THC = 0 ng/mL N-methyl-1-phenylpropan-2-amine = negative 7-AminoFlunitrazepam = negative
Jeff Chase	Serum Albumin = 3.5 g/dL Saffron extract = negative Creatinine = 59 umol/L Glucose = N/A 3'- azido-3'-deoxythymidine = negative Creatine phosphokinase = 135 U/L	BAC = 0.021% Cocaine = 0.00mg/L THC = 0 ng/mL N-methyl-1-phenylpropan-2-amine = negative 7-AminoFlunitrazepam = negative
Emit Purel	Serum Albumin = 2.4 g/dL Saffron extract = positive Creatinine = 71 umol/L Glucose = N/A 3'- azido-3'-deoxythymidine = negative Creatine phosphokinase = 179 U/L	BAC = 0.00% Cocaine = 0.00mg/L THC = 0 ng/mL N-methyl-1-phenylpropan-2-amine = negative 7-AminoFlunitrazepam = positive
Karel Novak	Serum Albumin = 2.9 g/dL Saffron extract = positive Creatinine =118 umol/L Glucose = N/A 3'- azido-3'-deoxythymidine = negative Creatine phosphokinase = 185U/L	BAC = 0.00% Cocaine = 0.00mg/L THC = 0 ng/mL N-methyl-1-phenylpropan-2-amine = negative 7-AminoFlunitrazepam = negative
Kale Anderson	Serum Albumin = 3.9 g/dL Saffron extract = negative Creatinine = 58 umol/L Glucose = N/A 3'- azido-3'-deoxythymidine = negative Creatine phosphokinase = 184 U/L	BAC = 0.00% Cocaine = 0.00mg/L THC = 0 ng/mL N-methyl-1-phenylpropan-2-amine = negative 7-AminoFlunitrazepam = negative
Dr. Aster Greendale	Serum Albumin = 4.1 g/dL Saffron extract = negative Creatinine = 58 umol/L Glucose = N/A 3'- azido-3'-deoxythymidine = negative Creatine phosphokinase = 80 U/L	BAC = 0.017% Cocaine = 0.00mg/L THC = 0.21 ng/mL N-methyl-1-phenylpropan-2-amine = negative 7-AminoFlunitrazepam = negative

IMPORTANT: This report contains proprietary and original material. Accordingly, this document may not be copied or released to third parties without consent.

The Dolphin Hotel Murders
A Forensic Crime Scene Inquiry Lab

K.J. Sukhu

Constantine Ghibarivinova	Serum Albumin = 3.9 g/dL Saffron extract = negative Creatinine = 99 umol/L Glucose = N/A 3'- azido-3'-deoxythymidine = negative Creatine phosphokinase = 125 U/L	BAC = 0.017% Cocaine = 0.00mg/L THC = 0 ng/mL N-methyl-1-phenylpropan-2-amine = negative 7-AminoFlunitrazepam = negative
Hyeon Gi-Dong	Serum Albumin = 3.9 g/dL Saffron extract = negative Creatinine = 58 umol/L Glucose = N/A 3'- azido-3'-deoxythymidine = negative Creatine phosphokinase = 89 U/L	BAC = 0.021% Cocaine = 0.00mg/L THC = 0.24 ng/mL N-methyl-1-phenylpropan-2-amine = negative 7-AminoFlunitrazepam = negative
Nicholas Brenner	Serum Albumin = 4.1 g/dL Saffron extract = negative Creatinine = 65 umol/L Glucose = N/A 3'- azido-3'-deoxythymidine = negative Creatine phosphokinase = 160 U/L	BAC = 0.00% Cocaine = 0.00mg/L THC = 0 ng/mL N-methyl-1-phenylpropan-2-amine = negative 7-AminoFlunitrazepam = negative

The Dolphin Hotel Murders
A Forensic Crime Scene Inquiry Lab

K.J. Sukhu

Objects of Significance Recovered
The DNA was not cut properly and so bands appear on the same sample

The original scientist who took the DNA samples did not do such a thorough job. They only used one restriction enzyme and, in addition, mixed up the different bands among the suspects and the victims. You will have to unravel the mystery.

Note: For further assistance, please refer to the Appendix section entitled "How to Analyze DNA".

Victim 1

A female body was found burned beyond recognition. An autopsy showed that the cause of death was from multiple stab wounds and not the burning. The body showed little to no signs of restraint or struggle. The knife that fits the profile of the stab wounds was recovered and the DNA analyzed.

DNA recovered from Victim 1

Band	Mixed DNA
44	
38	
37	
36	
19	
16	
12	
11	
9	
6	

DNA recovered from the knife

Band	Mixed DNA
60	
44	
37	
33	
16	
12	
11	
9	
6	

The Dolphin Hotel Murders
A Forensic Crime Scene Inquiry Lab

Victim 2

What appears to be the remains of a male were found. The strange part is, major portions of the body were missing. Vital organs had been removed and chunks of flesh were missing from the corpse.

DNA recovered from Victim 2

Band	Mixed DNA
57	
46	
45	
38	
31	
30	
27	
25	
17	
8	
7	
3	

Victim 3

A corpse was found with the face removed. The corpse showed obvious signs of torture. Restraint marks were found on the hands and legs of the victim.

DNA recovered from Victim 3

Band	Mixed DNA
53	
43	
37	
34	
27	
26	
25	
24	
22	
16	
15	
13	
12	
10	
9	
8	
5	

The Dolphin Hotel Murders
A Forensic Crime Scene Inquiry Lab

K.J. Sukhu

Victim 4

A corpse was and has been rotting for months. It seems that the death must have been very early on in the storm. The body has stab marks in the back. The body also has small scratches which may indicate a futile struggle after the stabbing.

DNA recovered from Victim 4

Band	Mixed DNA
43	
32	
29	
25	
19	
16	
13	
12	
7	

Victim 5

It was determined that the victim died from internal bleeding. His ribs were broken and there were lacerations to his skull. His radius and ulna had fractures and he had bruising on his femur and tibia.

DNA recovered from Victim 5

Band	Mixed DNA
60	
54	
53	
48	
46	
37	
34	
33	
27	
26	
24	
20	
17	
15	
12	
11	
10	
9	
8	
7	
3	

The Dolphin Hotel Murders   K.J. Sukhu
A Forensic Crime Scene Inquiry Lab

Victim 6

The victim had signs of malnutrition and physical abuse. The abuse seemed to be ongoing until the victim finally succumbed to the violence.

DNA recovered from Victim 6

Band	Mixed DNA
53	
37	
35	
29	
15	
9	

Victim 7

The victim had no signs of abuse. There was no evidence of an altercation.

DNA recovered from Victim 7

Band	Mixed DNA
44	
43	
22	
5	

The Dolphin Hotel Murders
A Forensic Crime Scene Inquiry Lab

K.J. Sukhu

Map of Floor 14:
This map is incomplete. You must complete it.

The 14th floor has undergone changes since the storm hit. You must identify any special rooms, identify all room numbers as well as ascertain which guest stayed in which room.

The Dolphin Hotel Murders
A Forensic Crime Scene Inquiry Lab

K.J. Sukhu

Rough Copy

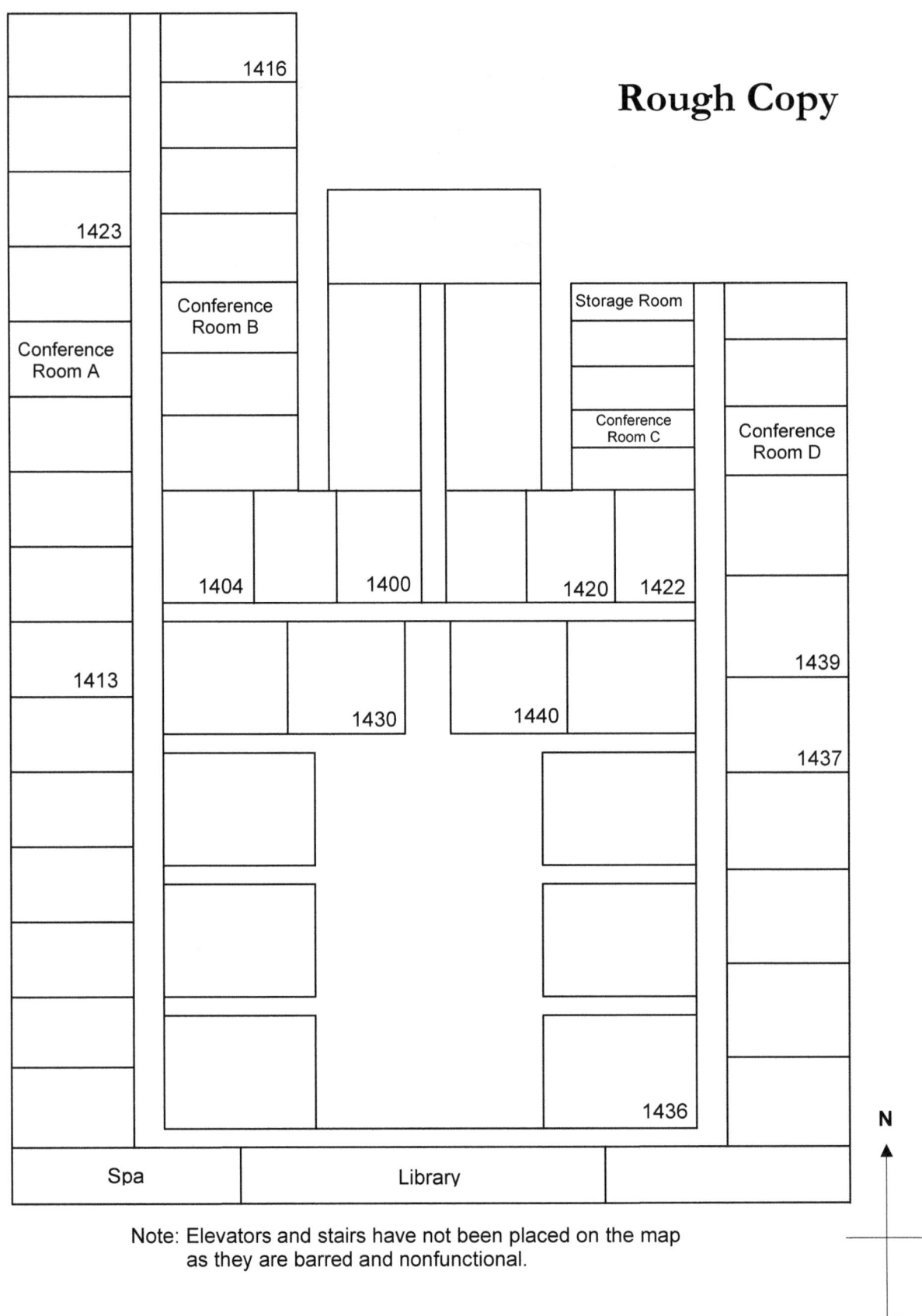

Note: Elevators and stairs have not been placed on the map as they are barred and nonfunctional.

N

IMPORTANT: This report contains proprietary and original material. Accordingly, this document may not be copied or released to third parties without consent.

The Dolphin Hotel Murders
A Forensic Crime Scene Inquiry Lab

K.J. Sukhu

Good Copy

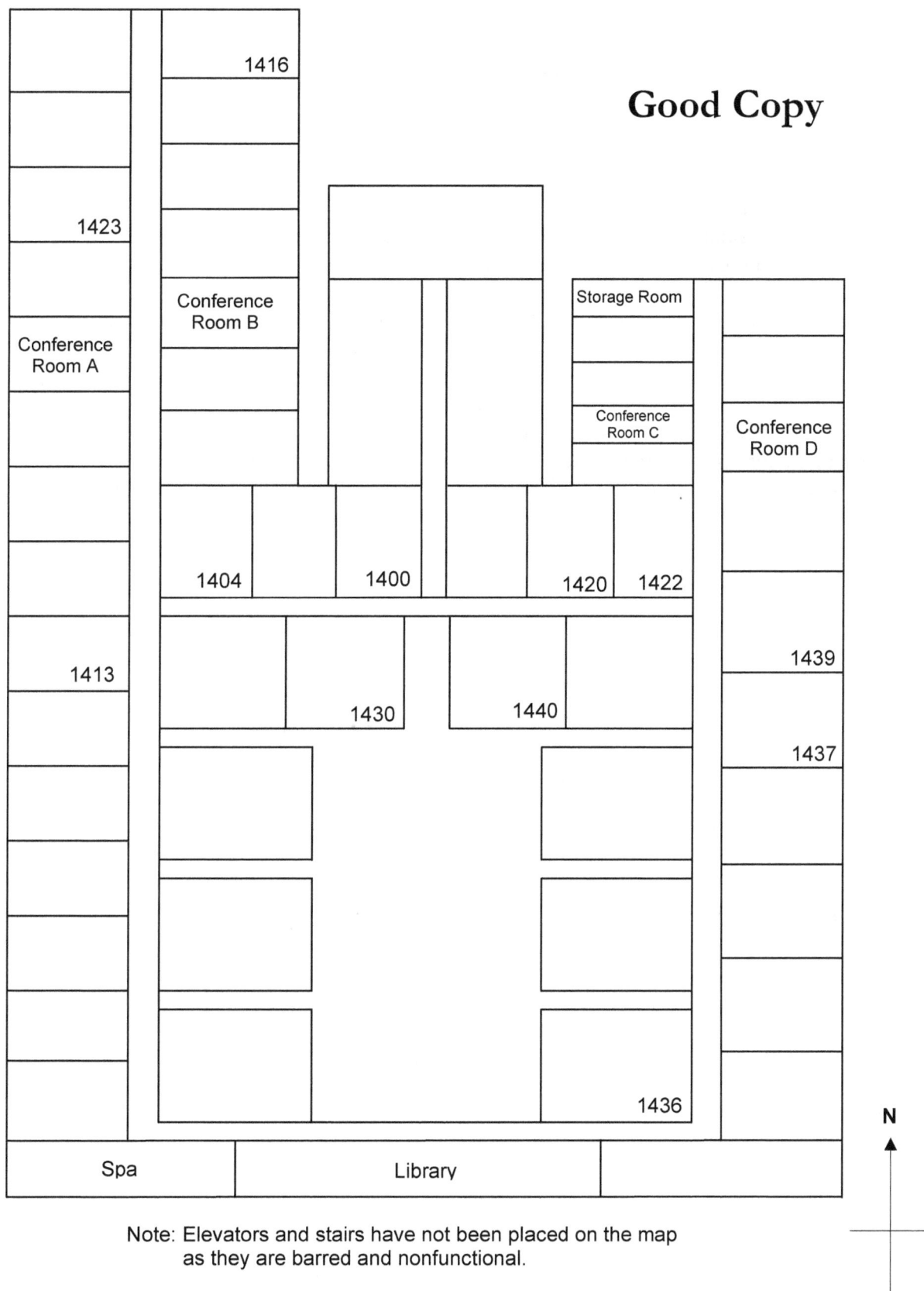

Note: Elevators and stairs have not been placed on the map as they are barred and nonfunctional.

IMPORTANT: This report contains proprietary and original material. Accordingly, this document may not be copied or released to third parties without consent.

The Dolphin Hotel Murders
A Forensic Crime Scene Inquiry Lab

K.J. Sukhu

DNA Analysis
DNA provided for all residents of Floor 14

Use the restriction enzyme to put all residents' DNA into bands. Cross reference all the bands with the DNA samples found on the victims. Use the knowledge you've gained in the story to figure out who the murderer(s) is/are and who are the actual victims.

Note: To see how to properly "cut" your DNA refer to the Appendix section entitled "How to Cut DNA".

To cut the DNA you will use the restriction enzyme "Fay-KE". Look for the exact DNA pattern and cut only where instructed to (Figure 4-1). Remember that fragments are considered to be continuous (think of the 6 pieces as one long strand of DNA). Make sure you correctly identify all the areas to cut or your DNA bands will be incorrect.

Restriction Enzyme Fay-KE

$$\begin{array}{c} CG \\ CG \\ TA \\ \hline AT \\ GC \\ GC \end{array} \text{Cut Here}$$

Figure 4-1

IMPORTANT: This report contains proprietary and original material. Accordingly, this document may not be copied or released to third parties without consent.

The Dolphin Hotel Murders
A Forensic Crime Scene Inquiry Lab

K.J. Sukhu

Nikolai Astafurov

1	2	3	4	5	6
C-G	G-C	A-T	A-T	T-A	C-G
C-G	T-A	C-G	A-T	T-A	C-G
T-A	T-A	A-T	G-C	G-C	T-A
A-T	G-C	A-T	A-T	C-G	A-T
G-C	C-G	A-T	C-G	A-T	G-C
G-C	A-T	G-C	A-T	C-G	G-C
G-C	C-G	C-G	C-G	A-T	T-A
T-A	A-T	G-C	C-G	A-T	G-C
T-A	A-T	T-A	T-A	A-T	C-G
G-C	A-T	T-A	A-T	G-C	A-T
C-G	G-C	A-T	G-C	T-A	C-G
A-T	C-G	C-G	G-C	T-A	A-T
A-T	G-C	A-T	A-T	A-T	A-T
A-T	T-A	A-T	A-T	C-G	A-T
G-C	T-A	A-T	A-T	A-T	G-C
C-G	G-C	G-C	G-C	A-T	T-A
A-T	C-G	C-G	C-G	A-T	T-A
T-A	G-C	G-C	G-C	G-C	A-T
G-C	T-A	T-A	T-A	C-G	C-G

Band #	DNA

Kim Ye Park

1	2	3	4	5	6
T-A	T-A	T-A	G-C	C-G	C-G
T-A	T-A	G-C	C-G	C-G	A-T
T-A	G-C	C-G	A-T	T-A	C-G
G-C	C-G	A-T	C-G	A-T	A-T
C-G	A-T	C-G	A-T	G-C	A-T
A-T	C-G	C-G	A-T	G-C	A-T
C-G	A-T	A-T	A-T	C-G	G-C
A-T	A-T	A-T	G-C	A-T	T-A
A-T	A-T	A-T	T-A	C-G	T-A
A-T	G-C	C-G	T-A	A-T	A-T
G-C	T-A	C-G	A-T	A-T	C-G
T-A	T-A	T-A	C-G	A-T	A-T
C-G	A-T	A-T	A-T	G-C	T-A
C-G	C-G	G-C	T-A	T-A	G-C
T-A	A-T	G-C	T-A	T-A	C-G
A-T	A-T	A-T	G-C	A-T	A-T
G-C	A-T	G-C	C-G	C-G	C-G
G-C	G-C	C-G	A-T	A-T	A-T
C-G	C-G	T-A	C-G	T-A	A-T

Band #	DNA

The Dolphin Hotel Murders
A Forensic Crime Scene Inquiry Lab

K.J. Sukhu

Ghobad Farshad

1	2	3	4	5	6
A-T	A-T	T-A	T-A	T-A	C-G
G-C	G-C	T-A	A-T	T-A	C-G
T-A	T-A	G-C	C-G	G-C	T-A
T-A	T-A	C-G	A-T	C-G	A-T
A-T	C-G	A-T	T-A	A-T	G-C
C-G	C-G	C-G	T-A	C-G	G-C
A-T	T-A	A-T	G-C	A-T	A-T
T-A	A-T	A-T	C-G	C-G	C-G
T-A	G-C	A-T	A-T	C-G	A-T
G-C	G-C	G-C	C-G	T-A	A-T
C-G	C-G	T-A	A-T	A-T	A-T
A-T	A-T	T-A	C-G	G-C	G-C
C-G	A-T	A-T	A-T	G-C	C-G
A-T	A-T	C-G	A-T	A-T	C-G
C-G	G-C	A-T	A-T	G-C	T-A
A-T	C-G	A-T	G-C	A-T	A-T
A-T	A-T	A-T	A-T	G-C	G-C
A-T	C-G	G-C	G-C	C-G	G-C
G-C	A-T	C-G	C-G	C-G	A-T

Band #	DNA

Loyan Sheik

1	2	3	4	5	6
C-G	G-C	A-T	G-C	G-C	G-C
C-G	T-A	C-G	C-G	T-A	T-A
T-A	T-A	A-T	C-G	T-A	T-A
A-T	A-T	A-T	T-A	G-C	G-C
G-C	C-G	A-T	A-T	C-G	C-G
G-C	A-T	G-C	G-C	A-T	A-T
G-C	A-T	C-G	G-C	C-G	C-G
T-A	A-T	G-C	G-C	A-T	A-T
T-A	G-C	T-A	T-A	A-T	A-T
A-T	A-T	T-A	T-A	A-T	C-G
C-G	G-C	A-T	A-T	G-C	C-G
C-G	C-G	C-G	C-G	C-G	T-A
T-A	C-G	A-T	A-T	G-C	A-T
A-T	A-T	A-T	A-T	T-A	G-C
G-C	G-C	A-T	A-T	T-A	G-C
G-C	C-G	G-C	G-C	G-C	G-C
C-G	G-C	C-G	C-G	C-G	C-G
A-T	T-A	G-C	G-C	G-C	G-C
G-C	C-G	T-A	G-C	T-A	T-A

Band #	DNA

IMPORTANT: This report contains proprietary and original material. Accordingly, this document may not be copied or released to third parties without consent.

The Dolphin Hotel Murders
A Forensic Crime Scene Inquiry Lab

K.J. Sukhu

Raza Jehanzib

1	2	3	4	5	6
T-A	G-C	C-G	G-C	A-T	G-C
G-C	T-A	C-G	C-G	C-G	C-G
C-G	T-A	T-A	A-T	A-T	A-T
G-C	G-C	A-T	C-G	A-T	C-G
T-A	C-G	G-C	A-T	A-T	C-G
C-G	A-T	G-C	A-T	G-C	C-G
C-G	C-G	C-G	A-T	C-G	T-A
T-A	A-T	A-T	G-C	C-G	A-T
A-T	A-T	A-T	T-A	T-A	G-C
G-C	A-T	A-T	T-A	A-T	G-C
G-C	G-C	G-C	A-T	G-C	C-G
A-T	C-G	C-G	C-G	G-C	A-T
C-G	G-C	G-C	A-T	A-T	A-T
A-T	T-A	T-A	T-A	T-A	A-T
A-T	T-A	G-C	T-A	T-A	G-C
A-T	G-C	C-G	G-C	G-C	T-A
G-C	C-G	G-C	C-G	C-G	T-A
C-G	G-C	T-A	A-T	T-A	A-T
T-A	T-A	C-G	C-G	G-C	C-G

Band #	DNA

Thien Vo Duong

1	2	3	4	5	6
A-T	C-G	G-C	C-G	G-C	A-T
A-T	C-G	T-A	A-T	T-A	A-T
G-C	T-A	T-A	C-G	T-A	G-C
C-G	A-T	G-C	A-T	G-C	C-G
G-C	G-C	C-G	A-T	C-G	C-G
T-A	G-C	A-T	A-T	A-T	T-A
T-A	C-G	C-G	G-C	C-G	A-T
G-C	A-T	A-T	C-G	A-T	G-C
C-G	A-T	A-T	G-C	A-T	G-C
G-C	C-G	A-T	T-A	A-T	G-C
T-A	C-G	G-C	G-C	G-C	T-A
T-A	T-A	C-G	C-G	C-G	G-C
G-C	A-T	G-C	G-C	G-C	C-G
C-G	G-C	T-A	T-A	T-A	G-C
A-T	G-C	T-A	T-A	T-A	T-A
C-G	G-C	G-C	G-C	G-C	G-C
A-T	C-G	C-G	C-G	C-G	C-G
A-T	G-C	G-C	G-C	G-C	G-C
A-T	A-T	T-A	A-T	T-A	A-T

Band #	DNA

The Dolphin Hotel Murders
A Forensic Crime Scene Inquiry Lab

K.J. Sukhu

Thishanth Senmugalingam

1	2	3	4	5	6
T-A	T-A	C-G	A-T	G-C	C-G
A-T	T-A	C-G	C-G	C-G	A-T
C-G	G-C	T-A	A-T	A-T	T-A
A-T	C-G	A-T	A-T	C-G	T-A
A-T	A-T	G-C	A-T	A-T	G-C
C-G	C-G	G-C	G-C	A-T	C-G
C-G	A-T	C-G	C-G	A-T	C-G
T-A	A-T	A-T	C-G	G-C	C-G
A-T	A-T	A-T	T-A	T-A	T-A
G-C	G-C	A-T	A-T	T-A	A-T
G-C	T-A	G-C	G-C	A-T	G-C
C-G	T-A	T-A	G-C	C-G	G-C
A-T	A-T	T-A	T-A	A-T	C-G
T-A	C-G	A-T	A-T	T-A	A-T
T-A	A-T	T-A	T-A	T-A	T-A
G-C	A-T	G-C	G-C	G-C	T-A
C-G	A-T	C-G	C-G	C-G	G-C
A-T	G-C	A-T	A-T	A-T	C-G
C-G	C-G	C-G	C-G	C-G	A-T

Band #	DNA

Wright Walker

1	2	3	4	5	6
G-C	G-C	A-T	A-T	G-C	C-G
C-G	T-A	C-G	C-G	T-A	C-G
A-T	T-A	C-G	A-T	T-A	T-A
C-G	G-C	C-G	A-T	G-C	A-T
A-T	C-G	C-G	A-T	C-G	G-C
A-T	A-T	T-A	A-T	A-T	G-C
A-T	C-G	A-T	A-T	C-G	C-G
G-C	C-G	G-C	A-T	A-T	A-T
T-A	G-C	G-C	G-C	A-T	A-T
T-A	T-A	C-G	C-G	A-T	A-T
A-T	C-G	A-T	C-G	G-C	G-C
C-G	C-G	C-G	T-A	C-G	T-A
A-T	T-A	A-T	A-T	G-C	T-A
T-A	A-T	A-T	G-C	T-A	A-T
T-A	G-C	A-T	G-C	T-A	C-G
G-C	G-C	G-C	T-A	G-C	A-T
C-G	T-A	C-G	G-C	C-G	T-A
A-T	T-A	G-C	C-G	G-C	T-A
C-G	G-C	T-A	G-C	T-A	G-C

Band #	DNA

The Dolphin Hotel Murders
A Forensic Crime Scene Inquiry Lab

K.J. Sukhu

William Fraiser

1	2	3	4	5	6
G-C	G-C	G-C	G-C	G-C	A-T
T-A	T-A	T-A	T-A	C-G	C-G
T-A	T-A	T-A	T-A	A-T	A-T
G-C	G-C	G-C	G-C	C-G	T-A
C-G	C-G	C-G	C-G	A-T	C-G
A-T	A-T	A-T	A-T	A-T	C-G
C-G	C-G	C-G	C-G	A-T	T-A
C-G	C-G	A-T	C-G	G-C	A-T
T-A	T-A	A-T	T-A	T-A	G-C
A-T	A-T	A-T	A-T	T-A	G-C
G-C	G-C	G-C	G-C	A-T	T-A
G-C	G-C	C-G	G-C	C-G	T-A
C-G	T-A	G-C	A-T	A-T	A-T
G-C	G-C	T-A	C-G	T-A	C-G
T-A	C-G	T-A	A-T	T-A	A-T
C-G	G-C	G-C	T-A	G-C	T-A
G-C	T-A	C-G	T-A	C-G	T-A
T-A	G-C	G-C	G-C	A-T	C-G
C-G	C-G	T-A	C-G	C-G	A-T

Band #	DNA

Nemo Renee

1	2	3	4	5	6
G-C	G-C	C-G	G-C	G-C	G-C
C-G	T-A	C-G	C-G	T-A	C-G
G-C	T-A	T-A	C-G	T-A	A-T
T-A	G-C	A-T	T-A	G-C	C-G
C-G	C-G	G-C	A-T	C-G	A-T
C-G	A-T	G-C	G-C	A-T	A-T
T-A	C-G	A-T	G-C	C-G	A-T
A-T	A-T	C-G	A-T	A-T	G-C
G-C	A-T	A-T	G-C	T-A	T-A
G-C	A-T	A-T	T-A	C-G	T-A
C-G	G-C	A-T	T-A	C-G	A-T
G-C	C-G	G-C	A-T	T-A	C-G
T-A	G-C	T-A	C-G	A-T	A-T
T-A	T-A	T-A	A-T	G-C	T-A
G-C	T-A	A-T	T-A	G-C	T-A
C-G	G-C	C-G	T-A	C-G	G-C
C-G	C-G	A-T	G-C	A-T	C-G
A-T	G-C	T-A	A-T	T-A	A-T
C-G	T-A	G-C	T-A	T-A	C-G

Band #	DNA

IMPORTANT: This report contains proprietary and original material. Accordingly, this document may not be copied or released to third parties without consent.

The Dolphin Hotel Murders
A Forensic Crime Scene Inquiry Lab

K.J. Sukhu

Emily Jones

1	2	3	4	5	6
A-T	C-G	A-T	G-C	G-C	G-C
G-C	C-G	A-T	T-A	C-G	C-G
G-C	T-A	G-C	T-A	A-T	A-T
A-T	A-T	G-C	G-C	C-G	C-G
C-G	G-C	C-G	C-G	C-G	A-T
C-G	G-C	C-G	A-T	T-A	A-T
T-A	A-T	T-A	C-G	A-T	A-T
A-T	C-G	A-T	A-T	G-C	G-C
G-C	A-T	G-C	A-T	G-C	T-A
G-C	A-T	G-C	A-T	T-A	T-A
T-A	A-T	A-T	G-C	A-T	A-T
A-T	G-C	A-T	C-G	C-G	C-G
C-G	C-G	G-C	G-C	A-T	A-T
A-T	G-C	C-G	T-A	T-A	T-A
T-A	T-A	G-C	T-A	T-A	T-A
T-A	T-A	T-A	G-C	G-C	G-C
G-C	G-C	T-A	C-G	C-G	C-G
C-G	C-G	T-A	G-C	T-A	A-T
T-A	G-C	G-C	T-A	G-C	C-G

Band #	DNA

Nick James Von Riemsdike

1	2	3	4	5	6
G-C	G-C	T-A	G-C	G-C	G-C
T-A	T-A	C-G	C-G	T-A	T-A
T-A	T-A	C-G	A-T	T-A	T-A
G-C	G-C	T-A	C-G	G-C	G-C
C-G	C-G	A-T	A-T	C-G	C-G
A-T	A-T	G-C	A-T	A-T	C-G
C-G	C-G	G-C	A-T	C-G	T-A
C-G	A-T	G-C	G-C	A-T	A-T
T-A	A-T	T-A	T-A	A-T	G-C
A-T	A-T	T-A	T-A	A-T	G-C
G-C	G-C	G-C	A-T	G-C	T-A
G-C	C-G	C-G	C-G	C-G	T-A
C-G	G-C	A-T	A-T	G-C	A-T
A-T	T-A	C-G	T-A	T-A	C-G
C-G	T-A	A-T	T-A	T-A	A-T
A-T	G-C	A-T	G-C	G-C	T-A
A-T	C-G	A-T	C-G	C-G	T-A
A-T	G-C	G-C	A-T	G-C	G-C
G-C	T-A	C-G	C-G	T-A	C-G

Band #	DNA

The Dolphin Hotel Murders
A Forensic Crime Scene Inquiry Lab

K.J. Sukhu

Ash Pikmin

1	2	3	4	5	6
G-C	A-T	G-C	G-C	G-C	G-C
C-G	A-T	T-A	C-G	C-G	C-G
A-T	G-C	T-A	A-T	C-G	A-T
C-G	C-G	G-C	C-G	T-A	C-G
A-T	G-C	C-G	A-T	A-T	A-T
A-T	T-A	A-T	A-T	G-C	A-T
C-G	T-A	C-G	A-T	G-C	A-T
C-G	G-C	A-T	G-C	G-C	G-C
T-A	C-G	A-T	T-A	T-A	T-A
A-T	G-C	A-T	T-A	T-A	T-A
G-C	T-A	G-C	A-T	A-T	A-T
G-C	A-T	C-G	C-G	C-G	C-G
A-T	C-G	G-C	A-T	A-T	C-G
G-C	A-T	T-A	T-A	A-T	C-G
T-A	A-T	T-A	T-A	G-C	T-A
G-C	A-T	G-C	G-C	T-A	A-T
C-G	G-C	C-G	C-G	T-A	G-C
G-C	C-G	G-C	A-T	A-T	G-C
T-A	G-C	T-A	C-G	C-G	A-T

Band #	DNA

Doctor Lee

1	2	3	4	5	6
G-C	G-C	C-G	G-C	C-G	A-T
C-G	T-A	G-C	C-G	C-G	A-T
A-T	T-A	T-A	A-T	T-A	G-C
C-G	G-C	T-A	C-G	A-T	C-G
A-T	C-G	G-C	A-T	G-C	G-C
A-T	A-T	C-G	A-T	G-C	T-A
A-T	C-G	G-C	A-T	G-C	T-A
A-T	A-T	C-G	G-C	C-G	G-C
A-T	A-T	G-C	T-A	G-C	C-G
A-T	A-T	T-A	T-A	T-A	G-C
G-C	G-C	C-G	A-T	A-T	T-A
C-G	C-G	C-G	C-G	C-G	A-T
C-G	G-C	T-A	A-T	A-T	C-G
T-A	T-A	A-T	T-A	A-T	A-T
A-T	T-A	G-C	T-A	A-T	A-T
G-C	G-C	G-C	G-C	G-C	A-T
G-C	C-G	G-C	C-G	C-G	G-C
C-G	G-C	T-A	A-T	A-T	C-G
A-T	T-A	T-A	C-G	C-G	G-C

Band #	DNA

The Dolphin Hotel Murders
A Forensic Crime Scene Inquiry Lab

K.J. Sukhu

Nicholas Brenner

1	2	3	4	5	6
T-A	G-C	G-C	G-C	A-T	G-C
T-A	C-G	C-G	T-A	A-T	C-G
A-T	A-T	A-T	T-A	G-C	C-G
C-G	C-G	C-G	G-C	C-G	T-A
A-T	A-T	A-T	C-G	G-C	A-T
T-A	A-T	C-G	A-T	T-A	G-C
C-G	A-T	C-G	C-G	T-A	G-C
C-G	G-C	T-A	A-T	G-C	A-T
T-A	T-A	A-T	A-T	C-G	C-G
A-T	T-A	G-C	A-T	G-C	A-T
G-C	A-T	G-C	G-C	T-A	A-T
G-C	C-G	G-C	C-G	A-T	A-T
C-G	A-T	C-G	G-C	C-G	G-C
G-C	T-A	G-C	T-A	A-T	C-G
T-A	T-A	T-A	T-A	A-T	G-C
A-T	G-C	A-T	G-C	A-T	T-A
C-G	C-G	C-G	C-G	G-C	T-A
A-T	A-T	A-T	G-C	C-G	G-C
A-T	C-G	A-T	T-A	G-C	C-G

Band #	DNA

Chevar Timothy Morrison

1	2	3	4	5	6
A-T	G-C	G-C	C-G	A-T	G-C
G-C	C-G	T-A	G-C	C-G	C-G
T-A	A-T	T-A	T-A	A-T	A-T
T-A	C-G	G-C	T-A	C-G	C-G
A-T	A-T	C-G	G-C	C-G	A-T
C-G	A-T	A-T	C-G	T-A	A-T
A-T	A-T	C-G	C-G	A-T	A-T
T-A	G-C	A-T	T-A	G-C	G-C
C-G	T-A	A-T	A-T	G-C	C-G
C-G	T-A	A-T	G-C	T-A	C-G
T-A	A-T	G-C	G-C	T-A	T-A
A-T	C-G	C-G	A-T	G-C	A-T
G-C	A-T	G-C	G-C	C-G	G-C
G-C	T-A	T-A	T-A	A-T	G-C
A-T	T-A	T-A	T-A	C-G	T-A
C-G	G-C	G-C	A-T	A-T	G-C
A-T	C-G	C-G	C-G	A-T	C-G
T-A	A-T	G-C	A-T	A-T	G-C
T-A	C-G	T-A	T-A	G-C	T-A

Band #	DNA

The Dolphin Hotel Murders
A Forensic Crime Scene Inquiry Lab

K.J. Sukhu

Zuzana Holubova

1	2	3	4	5	6
G-C	G-C	G-C	G-C	G-C	G-C
C-G	C-G	T-A	T-A	T-A	T-A
A-T	A-T	T-A	C-G	T-A	T-A
C-G	C-G	G-C	C-G	G-C	G-C
A-T	A-T	C-G	T-A	C-G	C-G
A-T	C-G	A-T	A-T	A-T	A-T
A-T	C-G	C-G	G-C	C-G	C-G
G-C	T-A	A-T	G-C	C-G	A-T
T-A	A-T	A-T	A-T	T-A	A-T
T-A	G-C	C-G	G-C	A-T	A-T
A-T	G-C	C-G	T-A	G-C	G-C
C-G	A-T	T-A	T-A	G-C	C-G
A-T	A-T	A-T	A-T	G-C	G-C
T-A	G-C	G-C	C-G	T-A	T-A
T-A	C-G	G-C	A-T	T-A	T-A
G-C	G-C	G-C	T-A	A-T	G-C
C-G	T-A	T-A	T-A	C-G	C-G
A-T	T-A	T-A	G-C	A-T	G-C
C-G	T-A	G-C	T-A	T-A	T-A

Band #	DNA

Femi Imami Kato

1	2	3	4	5	6
G-C	G-C	G-C	T-A	T-A	T-A
T-A	T-A	T-A	G-C	T-A	T-A
T-A	T-A	T-A	C-G	G-C	G-C
G-C	G-C	G-C	C-G	C-G	C-G
C-G	C-G	C-G	T-A	A-T	A-T
G-C	A-T	A-T	A-T	G-C	G-C
T-A	C-G	C-G	G-C	C-G	C-G
C-G	A-T	A-T	G-C	C-G	G-C
C-G	A-T	A-T	T-A	C-G	T-A
T-A	A-T	C-G	A-T	T-A	A-T
A-T	G-C	C-G	G-C	A-T	G-C
G-C	C-G	T-A	C-G	G-C	C-G
G-C	G-C	A-T	G-C	G-C	G-C
A-T	T-A	G-C	T-A	T-A	T-A
C-G	T-A	G-C	T-A	T-A	T-A
A-T	G-C	C-G	G-C	G-C	G-C
A-T	C-G	G-C	C-G	C-G	C-G
A-T	G-C	T-A	G-C	G-C	G-C
G-C	T-A	T-A	T-A	T-A	T-A

Band #	DNA

The Dolphin Hotel Murders
A Forensic Crime Scene Inquiry Lab

K.J. Sukhu

Nicholas Carter Bright III

1	2	3	4	5	6
G-C	C-G	T-A	C-G	T-A	T-A
T-A	G-C	C-G	G-C	T-A	T-A
T-A	T-A	C-G	T-A	C-G	G-C
G-C	A-T	T-A	A-T	C-G	C-G
C-G	G-C	A-T	G-C	T-A	A-T
A-T	C-G	G-C	C-G	A-T	G-C
C-G	C-G	G-C	A-T	G-C	C-G
A-T	C-G	A-T	C-G	G-C	G-C
A-T	T-A	A-T	C-G	A-T	T-A
A-T	A-T	A-T	T-A	A-T	A-T
G-C	G-C	G-C	A-T	A-T	G-C
C-G	G-C	C-G	G-C	G-C	C-G
G-C	A-T	G-C	G-C	C-G	G-C
T-A	G-C	T-A	T-A	G-C	T-A
T-A	C-G	T-A	T-A	T-A	T-A
G-C	G-C	G-C	G-C	T-A	G-C
C-G	T-A	G-C	C-G	G-C	C-G
G-C	T-A	T-A	G-C	G-C	G-C
T-A	G-C	C-G	T-A	T-A	T-A

Band #	DNA

Kieren Flynn

1	2	3	4	5	6
T-A	G-C	T-A	A-T	G-C	G-C
G-C	C-G	T-A	G-C	C-G	T-A
C-G	A-T	G-C	C-G	A-T	T-A
C-G	C-G	C-G	G-C	C-G	G-C
T-A	A-T	A-T	T-A	A-T	C-G
A-T	C-G	G-C	T-A	A-T	A-T
G-C	C-G	C-G	G-C	A-T	C-G
G-C	T-A	G-C	C-G	G-C	A-T
A-T	A-T	T-A	G-C	T-A	A-T
A-T	G-C	A-T	C-G	T-A	A-T
A-T	G-C	G-C	G-C	A-T	G-C
G-C	G-C	C-G	C-G	C-G	C-G
T-A	C-G	G-C	C-G	A-T	G-C
T-A	A-T	T-A	T-A	T-A	T-A
A-T	G-C	T-A	A-T	T-A	T-A
C-G	C-G	G-C	G-C	G-C	G-C
A-T	G-C	C-G	G-C	C-G	C-G
T-A	T-A	G-C	A-T	A-T	G-C
T-A	A-T	T-A	C-G	C-G	T-A

Band #	DNA

The Dolphin Hotel Murders
A Forensic Crime Scene Inquiry Lab

K.J. Sukhu

Jorgen Himmler

1	2	3	4	5	6
G-C	T-A	T-A	G-C	A-T	T-A
C-G	T-A	T-A	C-G	C-G	A-T
C-G	G-C	C-G	A-T	C-G	C-G
T-A	C-G	C-G	C-G	C-G	A-T
A-T	A-T	T-A	A-T	T-A	T-A
G-C	G-C	A-T	A-T	A-T	T-A
G-C	C-G	G-C	A-T	G-C	A-T
T-A	G-C	G-C	G-C	G-C	C-G
A-T	T-A	A-T	T-A	T-A	C-G
C-G	A-T	C-G	T-A	A-T	C-G
A-T	G-C	T-A	A-T	C-G	T-A
T-A	C-G	A-T	C-G	A-T	A-T
T-A	G-C	C-G	A-T	T-A	G-C
G-C	T-A	A-T	T-A	T-A	G-C
T-A	T-A	T-A	T-A	T-A	T-A
T-A	G-C	T-A	G-C	G-C	G-C
G-C	C-G	A-T	C-G	C-G	C-G
C-G	G-C	C-G	A-T	A-T	A-T
T-A	T-A	G-C	C-G	T-A	C-G

Band #	DNA

Laurent Abasi

1	2	3	4	5	6
T-A	T-A	T-A	G-C	A-T	T-A
T-A	T-A	T-A	C-G	C-G	A-T
A-T	G-C	C-G	A-T	C-G	C-G
C-G	C-G	C-G	C-G	C-G	A-T
A-T	A-T	T-A	A-T	T-A	T-A
T-A	G-C	A-T	A-T	A-T	T-A
T-A	C-G	G-C	C-G	G-C	A-T
G-C	G-C	G-C	C-G	G-C	C-G
C-G	T-A	A-T	T-A	T-A	C-G
A-T	A-T	C-G	A-T	A-T	C-G
C-G	G-C	T-A	G-C	C-G	T-A
G-C	C-G	A-T	G-C	A-T	A-T
T-A	G-C	C-G	A-T	T-A	G-C
T-A	T-A	C-G	T-A	T-A	G-C
G-C	T-A	T-A	T-A	T-A	T-A
C-G	G-C	A-T	G-C	G-C	G-C
G-C	C-G	G-C	C-G	C-G	C-G
T-A	G-C	G-C	A-T	A-T	A-T
G-C	T-A	G-C	C-G	T-A	C-G

Band #	DNA

IMPORTANT: This report contains proprietary and original material. Accordingly, this document may not be copied or released to third parties without consent.

The Dolphin Hotel Murders
A Forensic Crime Scene Inquiry Lab

K.J. Sukhu

Benny Heidmen

1	2	3	4	5	6
T-A	A-T	T-A	G-C	A-T	T-A
T-A	C-G	T-A	C-G	C-G	A-T
A-T	C-G	G-C	A-T	C-G	C-G
C-G	C-G	C-G	C-G	C-G	A-T
C-G	T-A	A-T	A-T	T-A	T-A
C-G	A-T	G-C	A-T	A-T	T-A
T-A	G-C	C-G	A-T	G-C	A-T
A-T	G-C	G-C	G-C	G-C	C-G
G-C	T-A	T-A	C-G	T-A	C-G
G-C	A-T	A-T	G-C	A-T	C-G
C-G	C-G	G-C	T-A	C-G	T-A
G-C	A-T	C-G	A-T	A-T	A-T
T-A	T-A	G-C	A-T	T-A	G-C
T-A	T-A	T-A	T-A	T-A	G-C
G-C	T-A	T-A	T-A	T-A	T-A
C-G	G-C	G-C	G-C	G-C	G-C
G-C	C-G	C-G	C-G	C-G	C-G
T-A	A-T	G-C	A-T	A-T	A-T
G-C	T-A	T-A	C-G	T-A	C-G

Band #	DNA

Rohit Mahajan

1	2	3	4	5	6
A-T	G-C	A-T	G-C	G-C	G-C
A-T	T-A	G-C	C-G	T-A	C-G
A-T	A-T	G-C	A-T	T-A	A-T
G-C	A-T	C-G	C-G	G-C	C-G
C-G	T-A	A-T	A-T	C-G	A-T
G-C	T-A	G-C	A-T	A-T	A-T
T-A	G-C	C-G	A-T	C-G	A-T
C-G	C-G	G-C	G-C	A-T	G-C
G-C	A-T	T-A	C-G	A-T	C-G
T-A	C-G	A-T	C-G	A-T	G-C
A-T	T-A	G-C	T-A	G-C	T-A
A-T	A-T	C-G	A-T	C-G	A-T
T-A	A-T	G-C	G-C	G-C	A-T
T-A	T-A	T-A	G-C	T-A	T-A
G-C	T-A	T-A	T-A	T-A	T-A
C-G	G-C	G-C	G-C	G-C	G-C
A-T	C-G	C-G	C-G	C-G	C-G
A-T	C-G	G-C	A-T	G-C	A-T
C-G	T-A	T-A	C-G	T-A	C-G

Band #	DNA

The Dolphin Hotel Murders
A Forensic Crime Scene Inquiry Lab

K.J. Sukhu

Ivan Restrepo Gil

1	2	3	4	5	6
C-G	A-T	A-T	A-T	C-G	G-C
A-T	A-T	A-T	G-C	G-C	C-G
C-G	T-A	G-C	G-C	T-A	A-T
C-G	T-A	C-G	C-G	A-T	C-G
G-C	G-C	G-C	A-T	C-G	A-T
T-A	C-G	T-A	A-T	C-G	A-T
T-A	A-T	A-T	A-T	T-A	A-T
G-C	C-G	A-T	G-C	A-T	G-C
C-G	C-G	G-C	C-G	G-C	C-G
G-C	G-C	C-G	G-C	G-C	G-C
C-G	T-A	A-T	T-A	C-G	T-A
A-T	A-T	C-G	A-T	C-G	A-T
A-T	A-T	C-G	C-G	G-C	A-T
A-T	T-A	G-C	C-G	T-A	T-A
G-C	T-A	T-A	T-A	T-A	T-A
C-G	T-A	T-A	A-T	G-C	G-C
G-C	T-A	C-G	G-C	C-G	C-G
T-A	G-C	C-G	G-C	G-C	A-T
A-T	C-G	T-A	C-G	T-A	C-G

Band #	DNA

Hyeon Gi-Dong

1	2	3	4	5	6
T-A	C-G	A-T	C-G	A-T	C-G
T-A	C-G	A-T	C-G	A-T	C-G
G-C	T-A	T-A	T-A	A-T	T-A
C-G	A-T	T-A	A-T	G-C	A-T
A-T	G-C	G-C	G-C	C-G	G-C
C-G	G-C	C-G	G-C	G-C	G-C
T-A	G-C	A-T	A-T	T-A	A-T
G-C	C-G	C-G	G-C	A-T	C-G
C-G	G-C	T-A	C-G	A-T	A-T
A-T	T-A	G-C	G-C	T-A	A-T
C-G	A-T	C-G	T-A	T-A	A-T
T-A	A-T	A-T	A-T	G-C	G-C
G-C	T-A	C-G	A-T	A-T	C-G
C-G	A-T	T-A	T-A	T-A	G-C
A-T	A-T	A-T	T-A	T-A	T-A
C-G	T-A	A-T	G-C	G-C	A-T
T-A	T-A	T-A	C-G	C-G	A-T
C-G	G-C	T-A	A-T	A-T	C-G
A-T	C-G	G-C	C-G	C-G	C-G

Band #	DNA

The Dolphin Hotel Murders
A Forensic Crime Scene Inquiry Lab

K.J. Sukhu

Constantine Ghibarivinova

1	2	3	4	5	6
C-G	A-T	A-T	G-C	C-G	G-C
C-G	A-T	A-T	C-G	G-C	C-G
C-G	T-A	G-C	A-T	T-A	C-G
T-A	T-A	C-G	C-G	A-T	C-G
A-T	G-C	G-C	A-T	A-T	T-A
G-C	C-G	C-G	A-T	T-A	A-T
G-C	A-T	C-G	A-T	T-A	G-C
G-C	C-G	T-A	G-C	G-C	G-C
C-G	C-G	A-T	C-G	C-G	C-G
G-C	G-C	G-C	G-C	A-T	G-C
C-G	T-A	G-C	T-A	C-G	T-A
A-T	A-T	C-G	A-T	C-G	A-T
A-T	A-T	C-G	A-T	G-C	C-G
A-T	C-G	G-C	T-A	T-A	C-G
G-C	C-G	T-A	T-A	T-A	T-A
C-G	T-A	T-A	G-C	G-C	A-T
G-C	A-T	G-C	C-G	C-G	G-C
T-A	G-C	T-A	A-T	G-C	G-C
A-T	G-C	A-T	C-G	T-A	C-G

Band #	DNA

Anthony Emmerson

1	2	3	4	5	6
T-A	C-G	A-T	G-C	A-T	C-G
T-A	A-T	G-C	C-G	A-T	C-G
G-C	C-G	G-C	C-G	A-T	T-A
C-G	A-T	T-A	C-G	G-C	A-T
A-T	A-T	G-C	T-A	C-G	G-C
C-G	A-T	C-G	A-T	G-C	G-C
T-A	G-C	A-T	G-C	T-A	A-T
G-C	C-G	C-G	G-C	A-T	C-G
C-G	G-C	T-A	C-G	A-T	A-T
C-G	T-A	G-C	G-C	T-A	A-T
C-G	A-T	C-G	T-A	T-A	A-T
T-A	A-T	A-T	A-T	G-C	G-C
A-T	T-A	C-G	A-T	A-T	C-G
G-C	A-T	T-A	T-A	T-A	G-C
G-C	A-T	A-T	T-A	T-A	T-A
C-G	T-A	A-T	G-C	G-C	A-T
T-A	C-G	T-A	C-G	C-G	A-T
C-G	C-G	T-A	A-T	A-T	C-G
A-T	T-A	G-C	C-G	C-G	C-G

Band #	DNA

The Dolphin Hotel Murders
A Forensic Crime Scene Inquiry Lab

K.J. Sukhu

Jamie Emmerson

1	2	3	4	5	6
T-A	C-G	A-T	G-C	A-T	G-C
T-A	A-T	C-G	C-G	A-T	C-G
G-C	C-G	C-G	A-T	A-T	C-G
C-G	A-T	T-A	C-G	G-C	T-A
A-T	A-T	A-T	A-T	C-G	A-T
C-G	A-T	G-C	A-T	G-C	G-C
T-A	G-C	G-C	A-T	C-G	G-C
G-C	C-G	C-G	G-C	C-G	C-G
C-G	G-C	T-A	C-G	T-A	A-T
A-T	T-A	G-C	G-C	A-T	A-T
C-G	A-T	C-G	T-A	G-C	A-T
T-A	A-T	A-T	A-T	G-C	G-C
G-C	T-A	C-G	A-T	A-T	C-G
C-G	A-T	T-A	T-A	T-A	G-C
C-G	A-T	A-T	T-A	T-A	T-A
T-A	T-A	A-T	G-C	G-C	A-T
A-T	T-A	T-A	C-G	C-G	A-T
G-C	G-C	T-A	A-T	A-T	C-G
G-C	C-G	G-C	C-G	C-G	C-G

Band #	DNA

Aa'idah Jiyad

1	2	3	4	5	6
C-G	A-T	A-T	G-C	A-T	G-C
A-T	A-T	A-T	C-G	G-C	C-G
C-G	T-A	C-G	A-T	G-C	A-T
C-G	T-A	C-G	C-G	A-T	C-G
G-C	G-C	T-A	A-T	A-T	A-T
T-A	C-G	A-T	A-T	T-A	A-T
C-G	A-T	G-C	A-T	T-A	A-T
C-G	C-G	G-C	G-C	G-C	G-C
T-A	C-G	G-C	C-G	C-G	C-G
A-T	G-C	C-G	G-C	A-T	G-C
G-C	T-A	A-T	T-A	C-G	T-A
G-C	A-T	C-G	A-T	C-G	A-T
A-T	A-T	C-G	A-T	G-C	A-T
A-T	T-A	G-C	T-A	T-A	T-A
G-C	T-A	T-A	T-A	T-A	T-A
C-G	T-A	T-A	G-C	G-C	G-C
G-C	T-A	G-C	C-G	C-G	C-G
T-A	G-C	T-A	C-G	G-C	A-T
A-T	C-G	A-T	T-A	T-A	C-G

Band #	DNA

The Dolphin Hotel Murders
A Forensic Crime Scene Inquiry Lab

K.J. Sukhu

Maeva Xavier

1	2	3	4	5	6
A-T	C-G	G-C	G-C	A-T	C-G
T-A	G-C	C-G	C-G	A-T	C-G
G-C	T-A	A-T	A-T	T-A	T-A
C-G	A-T	C-G	C-G	T-A	A-T
A-T	A-T	C-G	A-T	G-C	G-C
C-G	T-A	G-C	A-T	C-G	G-C
C-G	T-A	T-A	A-T	A-T	A-T
G-C	G-C	C-G	G-C	C-G	G-C
C-G	C-G	C-G	C-G	C-G	C-G
C-G	A-T	T-A	G-C	G-C	G-C
T-A	C-G	A-T	T-A	T-A	T-A
A-T	C-G	G-C	A-T	A-T	A-T
G-C	G-C	G-C	A-T	A-T	A-T
G-C	T-A	G-C	T-A	C-G	T-A
T-A	T-A	C-G	T-A	C-G	T-A
T-A	G-C	G-C	G-C	T-A	G-C
T-A	C-G	C-G	C-G	A-T	C-G
G-C	G-C	G-C	A-T	G-C	A-T
C-G	T-A	T-A	C-G	G-C	C-G

Band #	DNA

Robin Campelli

1	2	3	4	5	6
C-G	A-T	A-T	G-C	C-G	G-C
A-T	A-T	A-T	C-G	G-C	C-G
C-G	T-A	G-C	A-T	T-A	A-T
C-G	T-A	C-G	C-G	A-T	C-G
C-G	G-C	G-C	A-T	A-T	C-G
T-A	C-G	T-A	A-T	T-A	C-G
A-T	A-T	A-T	A-T	T-A	T-A
G-C	C-G	A-T	G-C	G-C	A-T
G-C	C-G	C-G	C-G	C-G	G-C
G-C	G-C	C-G	G-C	A-T	G-C
C-G	T-A	A-T	T-A	C-G	T-A
A-T	A-T	C-G	A-T	C-G	A-T
A-T	C-G	C-G	A-T	G-C	A-T
A-T	C-G	G-C	T-A	T-A	T-A
G-C	T-A	T-A	T-A	T-A	T-A
C-G	A-T	T-A	G-C	G-C	G-C
G-C	G-C	G-C	C-G	C-G	C-G
T-A	G-C	T-A	A-T	G-C	A-T
A-T	C-G	A-T	C-G	T-A	C-G

Band #	DNA

IMPORTANT: This report contains proprietary and original material. Accordingly, this document may not be copied or released to third parties without consent.

The Dolphin Hotel Murders
A Forensic Crime Scene Inquiry Lab

K.J. Sukhu

April McEwan

1	2	3	4	5	6
A-T	C-G	A-T	C-G	G-C	C-G
C-G	G-C	A-T	G-C	C-G	C-G
A-T	T-A	T-A	T-A	G-C	T-A
A-T	A-T	T-A	A-T	T-A	A-T
A-T	A-T	G-C	A-T	A-T	G-C
G-C	T-A	C-G	T-A	A-T	G-C
C-G	T-A	A-T	T-A	T-A	A-T
C-G	G-C	C-G	G-C	T-A	G-C
T-A	C-G	G-C	C-G	C-G	C-G
A-T	A-T	C-G	A-T	A-T	G-C
G-C	A-T	A-T	C-G	A-T	C-G
G-C	A-T	C-G	G-C	A-T	C-G
T-A	T-A	C-G	C-G	G-C	T-A
G-C	T-A	C-G	A-T	C-G	A-T
C-G	G-C	C-G	C-G	G-C	G-C
G-C	C-G	T-A	G-C	T-A	G-C
C-G	A-T	A-T	C-G	A-T	C-G
A-T	C-G	G-C	A-T	A-T	A-T
C-G	G-C	G-C	C-G	T-A	C-G

Band #	DNA

Adol Vice

1	2	3	4	5	6
C-G	A-T	A-T	G-C	C-G	G-C
A-T	C-G	A-T	C-G	G-C	C-G
C-G	C-G	G-C	A-T	T-A	A-T
C-G	T-A	C-G	C-G	A-T	C-G
G-C	A-T	G-C	A-T	A-T	C-G
T-A	G-C	T-A	A-T	T-A	T-A
T-A	G-C	A-T	A-T	T-A	A-T
G-C	C-G	A-T	G-C	G-C	G-C
C-G	C-G	G-C	C-G	C-G	C-G
G-C	G-C	C-G	G-C	A-T	G-C
C-G	T-A	A-T	C-G	C-G	T-A
A-T	A-T	C-G	C-G	C-G	A-T
A-T	A-T	C-G	T-A	G-C	A-T
A-T	T-A	C-G	A-T	T-A	T-A
G-C	T-A	T-A	G-C	T-A	T-A
C-G	T-A	A-T	G-C	G-C	G-C
G-C	T-A	G-C	C-G	C-G	C-G
T-A	G-C	G-C	A-T	G-C	A-T
A-T	C-G	A-T	C-G	T-A	C-G

Band #	DNA

IMPORTANT: This report contains proprietary and original material. Accordingly, this document may not be copied or released to third parties without consent.

The Dolphin Hotel Murders
A Forensic Crime Scene Inquiry Lab

K.J. Sukhu

Andrew Isaha Makai

1	2	3	4	5	6
A-T	C-G	A-T	C-G	G-C	G-C
C-G	C-G	A-T	G-C	C-G	C-G
A-T	T-A	T-A	T-A	G-C	A-T
A-T	A-T	T-A	A-T	C-G	C-G
A-T	G-C	G-C	A-T	C-G	A-T
G-C	G-C	C-G	T-A	T-A	A-T
C-G	T-A	A-T	T-A	A-T	A-T
G-C	G-C	C-G	G-C	G-C	G-C
T-A	C-G	C-G	C-G	G-C	C-G
A-T	A-T	T-A	A-T	A-T	G-C
A-T	A-T	A-T	C-G	A-T	T-A
T-A	A-T	G-C	G-C	A-T	C-G
T-A	T-A	G-C	C-G	G-C	C-G
G-C	T-A	G-C	A-T	C-G	T-A
C-G	G-C	T-A	C-G	G-C	A-T
G-C	C-G	T-A	G-C	T-A	G-C
C-G	A-T	G-C	C-G	A-T	G-C
A-T	C-G	T-A	A-T	A-T	A-T
C-G	G-C	A-T	C-G	T-A	C-G

Band #	DNA

Brigham Mosiah

1	2	3	4	5	6
C-G	C-G	A-T	G-C	A-T	G-C
C-G	A-T	A-T	C-G	A-T	C-G
T-A	C-G	T-A	A-T	A-T	C-G
A-T	C-G	T-A	C-G	G-C	T-A
G-C	C-G	G-C	A-T	C-G	A-T
G-C	T-A	C-G	A-T	G-C	G-C
T-A	A-T	A-T	A-T	T-A	G-C
G-C	G-C	C-G	G-C	A-T	C-G
C-G	G-C	T-A	C-G	A-T	A-T
A-T	T-A	G-C	G-C	T-A	A-T
C-G	A-T	C-G	T-A	T-A	A-T
T-A	A-T	A-T	A-T	G-C	G-C
G-C	T-A	C-G	A-T	C-G	C-G
C-G	A-T	T-A	T-A	C-G	G-C
A-T	A-T	A-T	T-A	T-A	T-A
C-G	T-A	A-T	G-C	A-T	A-T
T-A	T-A	T-A	C-G	G-C	A-T
C-G	G-C	T-A	A-T	G-C	C-G
A-T	C-G	G-C	C-G	C-G	C-G

Band #	DNA

The Dolphin Hotel Murders
A Forensic Crime Scene Inquiry Lab

K.J. Sukhu

Jeff Chase

1	2	3	4	5	6
A-T	C-G	A-T	C-G	G-C	G-C
C-G	G-C	C-G	G-C	C-G	C-G
A-T	T-A	C-G	T-A	G-C	A-T
A-T	A-T	T-A	A-T	T-A	C-G
C-G	A-T	A-T	A-T	A-T	A-T
C-G	T-A	G-C	T-A	A-T	A-T
T-A	T-A	G-C	T-A	T-A	A-T
A-T	G-C	C-G	G-C	T-A	G-C
G-C	C-G	G-C	C-G	C-G	C-G
G-C	A-T	C-G	A-T	C-G	G-C
A-T	A-T	A-T	C-G	C-G	T-A
T-A	A-T	C-G	G-C	T-A	A-T
T-A	T-A	C-G	C-G	A-T	A-T
G-C	C-G	G-C	A-T	G-C	T-A
C-G	C-G	T-A	C-G	G-C	T-A
G-C	T-A	T-A	G-C	T-A	G-C
C-G	A-T	G-C	C-G	A-T	C-G
A-T	G-C	T-A	A-T	A-T	A-T
C-G	G-C	A-T	C-G	T-A	C-G

Band #	DNA

Emit Purel

1	2	3	4	5	6
C-G	A-T	A-T	G-C	C-G	G-C
A-T	A-T	A-T	C-G	G-C	C-G
C-G	T-A	G-C	A-T	T-A	A-T
C-G	T-A	C-G	C-G	A-T	C-G
C-G	G-C	G-C	C-G	A-T	A-T
T-A	C-G	T-A	C-G	T-A	A-T
A-T	A-T	A-T	T-A	T-A	A-T
G-C	C-G	A-T	A-T	G-C	G-C
G-C	C-G	G-C	G-C	C-G	C-G
G-C	C-G	C-G	G-C	A-T	G-C
C-G	C-G	A-T	T-A	C-G	T-A
A-T	T-A	C-G	A-T	C-G	A-T
A-T	A-T	C-G	A-T	C-G	A-T
A-T	G-C	G-C	T-A	C-G	T-A
G-C	G-C	T-A	T-A	T-A	T-A
C-G	T-A	T-A	G-C	A-T	G-C
G-C	T-A	G-C	C-G	G-C	C-G
T-A	G-C	T-A	A-T	G-C	A-T
A-T	C-G	A-T	C-G	T-A	C-G

Band #	DNA

IMPORTANT: This report contains proprietary and original material. Accordingly, this document may not be copied or released to third parties without consent.

The Dolphin Hotel Murders
A Forensic Crime Scene Inquiry Lab

K.J. Sukhu

Karel Novak

1	2	3	4	5	6
A-T	C-G	A-T	C-G	G-C	C-G
C-G	C-G	A-T	G-C	C-G	C-G
A-T	T-A	T-A	T-A	G-C	T-A
A-T	A-T	C-G	A-T	T-A	A-T
A-T	G-C	C-G	A-T	A-T	G-C
G-C	G-C	T-A	T-A	A-T	G-C
C-G	T-A	A-T	T-A	T-A	A-T
G-C	G-C	G-C	G-C	T-A	G-C
T-A	C-G	G-C	C-G	C-G	C-G
A-T	A-T	C-G	A-T	A-T	G-C
A-T	A-T	A-T	C-G	A-T	T-A
T-A	A-T	C-G	G-C	A-T	A-T
T-A	T-A	C-G	C-G	C-G	A-T
G-C	T-A	G-C	A-T	C-G	T-A
C-G	G-C	T-A	C-G	T-A	T-A
G-C	C-G	T-A	G-C	A-T	G-C
C-G	A-T	G-C	C-G	G-C	C-G
A-T	C-G	T-A	A-T	G-C	A-T
C-G	G-C	A-T	C-G	T-A	C-G

Band #	DNA

Kale Anderson

1	2	3	4	5	6
C-G	A-T	A-T	G-C	C-G	G-C
A-T	G-C	A-T	C-G	G-C	C-G
C-G	G-C	G-C	A-T	T-A	A-T
C-G	T-A	C-G	C-G	A-T	C-G
G-C	C-G	G-C	A-T	A-T	C-G
T-A	C-G	T-A	A-T	T-A	T-A
T-A	T-A	A-T	A-T	T-A	A-T
G-C	A-T	A-T	G-C	G-C	G-C
C-G	G-C	G-C	C-G	C-G	G-C
G-C	G-C	C-G	C-G	A-T	G-C
C-G	T-A	A-T	C-G	C-G	T-A
A-T	A-T	C-G	T-A	C-G	A-T
A-T	A-T	C-G	A-T	G-C	A-T
A-T	T-A	G-C	G-C	T-A	T-A
G-C	T-A	T-A	G-C	T-A	T-A
C-G	T-A	T-A	G-C	G-C	G-C
C-G	T-A	G-C	C-G	C-G	C-G
C-G	G-C	T-A	A-T	G-C	A-T
T-A	C-G	A-T	C-G	T-A	C-G

Band #	DNA

The Dolphin Hotel Murders
A Forensic Crime Scene Inquiry Lab

K.J. Sukhu

Dr. Aster Greendale

1	2	3	4	5	6
C-G	A-T	A-T	G-C	C-G	G-C
C-G	A-T	C-G	C-G	G-C	C-G
T-A	T-A	C-G	A-T	T-A	A-T
A-T	T-A	T-A	C-G	A-T	C-G
G-C	G-C	A-T	A-T	A-T	A-T
G-C	C-G	G-C	A-T	T-A	A-T
T-A	A-T	G-C	A-T	T-A	A-T
G-C	C-G	A-T	G-C	G-C	G-C
C-G	C-G	G-C	C-G	C-G	C-G
G-C	G-C	C-G	G-C	C-G	G-C
C-G	T-A	A-T	T-A	T-A	T-A
A-T	A-T	C-G	A-T	A-T	A-T
A-T	C-G	C-G	A-T	G-C	A-T
A-T	C-G	G-C	T-A	G-C	T-A
G-C	T-A	T-A	T-A	T-A	T-A
C-G	A-T	T-A	G-C	G-C	G-C
G-C	G-C	G-C	C-G	C-G	C-G
T-A	G-C	T-A	A-T	G-C	A-T
A-T	C-G	A-T	C-G	T-A	C-G

Band #	DNA

IMPORTANT: This report contains proprietary and original material. Accordingly, this document may not be copied or released to third parties without consent.

The Dolphin Hotel Murders
A Forensic Crime Scene Inquiry Lab

K.J. Sukhu

What Do I Hand in?
After going through all the evidence you should come up with a solid case

The murderer(s) should be identified along with their motives, as well as all the victims. Cause of death should be revealed. All evidence to support your claims should also be presented.

1. Students will provide a detailed map/web of connections and relationships shared by the occupants of Floor 14. The more connections, the better. An example of a web is provided below (Figure 4-2).

Types of relationships may include (but are not limited to):
- Murderer/Victim
- Friendship
- Blood Relation
- Leadership
- Ideology
- Occupation

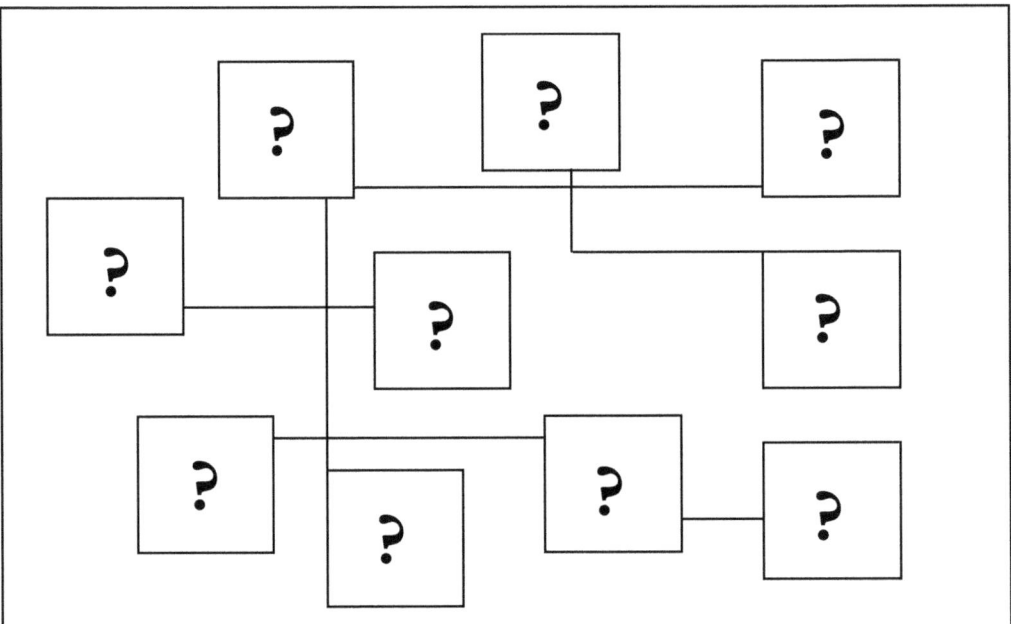

Figure 4-2

IMPORTANT: This report contains proprietary and original material. Accordingly, this document may not be copied or released to third parties without consent.

The Dolphin Hotel Murders
A Forensic Crime Scene Inquiry Lab

K.J. Sukhu

2. To accompany the visual relationship web, a detailed profile of the murderer(s) must be given.

This profile should include the following:
- A full explanation of the motive behind the murders.
- All available evidence that supports your accusation.

This may be written in paragraph form or may be put into a format such as the one shown below (Figure 4-3).

3. A detailed profile of each victim must be provided (Figure 4-4).

Figure 4-3

Profile — Murderer: ___ Age: ___ Gender: ___
Victim: ___
Motive: ___
Evidence: ___

Figure 4-4

Profile — Victim: ___ Age: ___ Gender: ___
Murdered By: ___
Cause of Death: ___
Evidence: ___

4. Any outlying "mysteries" surrounding the events at the Dolphin during the storm. This can be written in paragraph form.

The Dolphin Hotel Murders K.J. Sukhu
A Forensic Crime Scene Inquiry Lab

5. The 14th floor map including all room numbers, residents and any special rooms must be completed.

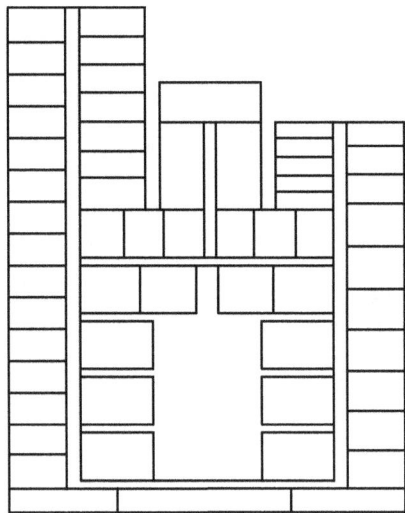

The Upper Crescent College Hockey Hazing Trial

A Court Case: Prosecution vs. Defense

The Upper Crescent College Hockey Hazing Trial
Prosecution vs. Defense

K.J. Sukhu

Introduction

Tradition, superstition and rituals have long been part of sport. They can be personal or a team practice. Usually traditions, superstitions and rituals are practiced to either facilitate team unity or give players a self perceived psychological edge over their opponent. While often having positive effects, their practices can also have negative consequences. When these rituals go beyond innocent intention, or are forced onto others, they can result in dividing teams rather than bringing them together. One such incident may have occurred involving the players on the Upper Crescent College (UCC) hockey team.

Mark Staffi, one of the members on the high school hockey team, recently suffered a serious injury which had allegedly occurred during a speculated hazing ritual. At the end of an unsupervised team practice, Mark suffered what doctors describe as "axial loading" of the L3-L5 portion of his spine. Mark's future playing career is uncertain. The season has been suspended and it is alleged that Mark was forced into a ritual by certain members of the team, which led to his injury. Most of his teammates deny the allegation, while some support his claim. It will be up to you to determine whether Mark's teammates (the defendants) are found to be innocent or should be held responsible for his injury.

This case, while not grabbing media attention, is being watched carefully by law makers, because the outcome of this trial may have repercussions for similar cases in the future.

As this case is very sensitive, only the best can be trusted and so this case has landed on your doorstep. You will either take the role of prosecutor and argue the guilt of the suspects (the other members of the hockey team) or you will take the role of a defense lawyer and argue their innocence (these choices may either be made by you or assigned by your instructor).

Whether you are on the side of the Defense team or the Prosecution it is important that you review all the information pertaining to the case.

The Information Available to You Includes

1. General Background Information
- This includes useful information regarding the school and its hockey program.

2. Team Biographies
- Profiles and alibis of the team members have been compiled.

3. Evidence
- Information and facts that will help prove either the innocence or guilt of the defendants.

4. Official Statements Taken by Investigators
- There are a few statements that investigators thought were significant enough to pass on to you.

5. The Phases of the Trial
- The trial consists of 5 phases; knowing what is expected of you may help you in your search for the truth.

The Upper Crescent College Hockey Hazing Trial
Prosecution vs. Defense

K.J. Sukhu

General Background Information
A look into the school and its hockey program

This information will give you a good foundation as to what might have led to the events. Although it may seem removed from the actual case, it's not.

Background Upper Crescent College (UCC) is one of the most "prestigious" all boys high schools in New Londo. It is a privately funded school and was built in 1923. It has a rich history. To attend UCC, tuition starts at $42,000 a year (which does not include books, supplies or uniforms). Preferential treatment is given to "legacy" students whose parents attended the school. UCC has a student population of 731 students ranging from grades 9-12.

The application alone is $450. Part of the admission process involves two separate interviews which are held with the prospective student and the parents. In addition, students write an aptitude test. Based on the cumulative scores and the availability of tuition, students may be offered admission.

About the School All sports, clubs and school activities are well supported by both the staff and the student body. However, the sports that garner the most attention are always lacrosse, hockey, football and basketball. The lacrosse and hockey teams have the longest running history at the school, dating back close to the school's establishment.

The Upper Ivy Hockey Association (UIHA) and the Upper Ivy Junior Hockey Association (UIJHA) The UIHA is a top tier league aimed at providing a premier hockey experience to high school aged students. Initially the UIHA amalgamated three of the "best" private school hockey leagues nationwide into one. There are now twenty schools currently involved with future plans to expand. Each school also has a junior team that plays in the UIJHA. Only students in grades 9-10 are eligible to play on the junior squad. The junior season is twelve games long. Students who are eligible may also play with their varsity team. The varsity team may use any enrolled students within the age limits of 13-19. The varsity teams play an extensive sixty game season (the most of any high school organization).

In order to be regarded as the top high school league, the UIHA also maintains a relegation penalty for the bottom two teams in each conference. The two lowest ranked teams at the end of the year are dropped from the league for a year and placed in a publicly run league. This provides ample motivation for teams to try their best to stay within the UIHA. Each regular season game has three periods. Period lengths are 15 minutes long with an additional overtime period provided if necessary. If a winner cannot be decided at the end of one overtime period, then a shoot-out is used to declare a winner. A win counts as two points, a loss in regulation yields zero points, but a loss in either overtime or a shootout yields one point. There are no "ties".

About the Program Hockey at UCC has a long standing tradition. "The players have a responsibility to the team, and the community has a responsibility to the team," said the athletic director. Every home game is always filled to capacity (the arena has a seating capacity of approximately 1000). "It would be impossible to just fill the arena with our students alone. Most of the time, family members of the players or students from the surrounding middle schools come to watch. It's a very popular community experience". The team is experiencing a transition year as the old coaching staff retired last year and a new coaching staff has taken over team operations.

Much of this information was taken before the season even began.

The Upper Crescent College Hockey Hazing Trial K.J. Sukhu
Prosecution vs. Defense

Team Biographies
Gain an insight into the characters you will either defend or prosecute

Knowing who you're defending or prosecuting is vital to your case. Proving or disproving their alibis is just as important.

The Team Roster

1. Jeff Fordice
2. Anthony Campelli
3. Steven Jae Wook
4. Mark Staffi
5. Paul Frasier
6. Scott McAferdy
7. Gerome Thompson
8. Matt Defrancesco
9. Wei Shien Gao
10. Austin Rodriguez
11. Brian Moore
12. Taylor Powell
13. Fitzgerald Stone
14. Neal Porter
15. Michael Bishop
16. Lucas Greene
17. Aiden Waters

	Team Depth Chart	
LW	**C**	**RW**
Anthony Campelli (A)	Jeff Fordice (C)	Paul Frasier
Gerome Thompson	Austin Rodriguez (A)	Aiden Waters
Matt Defrancesco	Steven Jae Wook	Wei Shien Gao
LD		**RD**
Taylor Powell		Lucas Greene
Brian Moore		Michael Bishop
Mark Staffi		Scott McAferdy
	G	
	Fitzgerald Stone	
	Neal Porter	

Post Selection Camp, Pre First Game

Coaches
18. Alistair Little – Head Coach
19. Anthony Garrett – Assistant Coach
20. Phillip McCoy – Assistant Coach

Jeff Fordice
Age: 18
Position: Centre, Captain

Background:
Jeff is a senior at UCC. This is his fourth year on the team but only his first as the team captain. Last year he wore the "A", but as the team lost most of their senior members upon graduation, giving Jeff the "C" was the obvious choice. He is a quiet person. His personality is much bigger on the ice than it is off the ice. His father is an alumni of UCC. His father is very proud of his son's accomplishments and often compares his "hockey accomplishments" to his own.

Alibi:
Elisabeth Leucete is Jeff's girlfriend. She claims that Jeff came back from practice to her house and that they went to a special midnight screening of "The Rocky Horror Show". Therefore, he couldn't have been at the rink when the incident occured. Elisabeth provided two movie tickets as evidence.

Anthony Campelli
Age: 18
Position: Left Wing, Assistant Captain

Background:
This is Anthony's fourth year at UCC and his third year on the team. He made the team in his second year and he's been quoted as saying that "it was one of the best things that happened [to him]". He is fiercely proud to wear the "A". At times he can become a little overzealous. He has a bit of an attitude and temper and has been on the verge of suspension for "on ice" incidents more than once.

Alibi:
Anthony says that he and Matt left "immediately" after practice, citing that it was past Matt's bedtime and they had school in the morning. He said normally they would "hang out" but, because Jeff was already leaving to go to the movies, they decided that there was really no point in staying. Therefore, he and Matt were not there when the incident took place. He stated that Matt ended up "crashing at his house" that evening.

Austin Rodriguez
Age: 17
Position: Center, Assistant Captain

Background:
This is Austin's second year on the team and first year as the assistant captain. He earned the "A" due to "a breakout performance" in his rookie year. Despite his youth, he

Alibi:
Austin says that everyone "was pretty tired after practice" and left shortly after. He's on record as saying that he, Michael and

managed to be one of the highest goal scorers on the team. He rapidly started attracting the attention of the coaches, which led to increased ice time throughout the season. By the end of the year he managed to work his way up to playing on the second line and was known as one of the "go to guys". He's been described as flamboyant, cocky, a smooth skater and a "natural born hockey player".

Paul all left the rink together to get a bite to eat. They produced a receipt to back up their claim.

Michael Bishop
Age: 18
Position: Defense

Background:
Michael is in his fourth year with the team. He made the squad as a forward on his first year of eligibility in grade nine. The coaching staff believed him to possess a very "raw talent" but they could see potential. Unfortunately, his first year was a major disappointment. The next year the coaching staff moved him to defense to see if that would spark a change. Once again, he had a disappointing year. He spent his third year on the lowest defensive pairing with reduced ice time. This year he's been moved up to the second defensive pairing based solely on his experience, however, expectations for him are not high.

Alibi:
Michael says that everyone "was pretty tired after practice" and left shortly after. He's on record as saying that he, Austin and Paul all left the rink together to get a bite to eat. They produced a receipt to back up their claim.

Scott McAferdy
Age: 14
Position: Defense

Background:
Scott is the youngest member on the team. He is in his first year of high school and his first year on the team. He is an enthusiastic young man and well liked by both his teammates and his classmates. His coaches are impressed with his "hockey IQ" as he usually makes

No Alibi:
Scott was at the rink when the incident occurred and was the one who contacted 911 about Mark's injuries. He claimed not to have actually seen the injury take place but alleges that most of the team was present and

	the right decisions on the ice. His teachers describe him as hardworking and a pleasure to teach. His marks are mostly A's and high B's.	aware of what happened at the time of the incident.
Aiden Waters Age:16 Position: Right Wing	**Background:** This is Aiden's first year at UCC but second year playing in the UIHA. He transferred from Highland Bishop Academy (HBA). Aiden is a good player, but unfortunately, this year HBA boasts one of the strongest lineups in the league. Because of this Aiden felt that staying at Bishop would result in a minuscule amount of playing time. To avoid this he transferred to UCC, where he receives plenty of ice time. The coaching staff has been impressed with him thus far and he is currently playing on the second line.	**Alibi:** Aiden claims that he left the rink at 10:45pm, even though the ice was booked until 11:00pm. He claims that his mom told him that he needed to be home and in bed by 11:30pm, so he left early.
Paul Frasier Age: 17 Position: Right Wing	**Background:** Paul is a hard working and dedicated member of the team. His height and physical play make him an imposing figure on the ice. The coaches use his intimidating stature to make space for his line mates. Because of this he is usually paired with skilled players and so he usually racks up assists throughout the year and ends up being one of the higher "point getters" on the team. Although he plays an important role, he hates his job. He wishes that the coaching staff would use him as an actual goal scorer rather than a "grinder".	**Alibi:** Paul says that everyone "was pretty tired after practice" and left shortly after. He's on record as saying that he, Michael and Austin all left the rink together to get a bite to eat. They produced a receipt to back up their claim.

Matt Defrancesco
Age: 15
Position: Left Wing

Background:
Matt is Anthony's cousin. He wasn't officially on the team the previous year, but because of his connection to Anthony he worked out and practiced with the team throughout the season. Impressed with his dedication and skill level, the coaching staff offered Matt a position on this year's team. He is a skilled skater, but his puck handling and decision making skills are a "work in progress" according to the coaching staff. Expectations are moderate.

Alibi:
Matt says that he and Anthony left "pretty quickly" after practice. He said that it was nearing his bedtime and they had school in the morning. He said normally they would "hang around" but because Jeff was leaving to go to the movies they decided to leave as well. He stated that he ended up "crashing at Anthony's house" that evening.

Gerome Thompson
Age: 16
Position: Left Wing

Background:
This is Gerome's first year with UCC. Gerome is a product of the "USA Under-17 Program". His eligibility within the program was just about to expire and so he was actively recruited to join UCC. Upon accepting, he was given a full scholarship. He chose to attend UCC because he figured he would get a "top-notch" education as opposed to a "neighborhood school" education as he puts it. He is a fantastic hockey player, but not the greatest student. He is still on-the-fence as to whether he plans to pursue a career in hockey or take a different route. The one thing he knows for sure though, is that hockey is his ticket to almost any college or university in the nation.

Alibi:
Gerome claims that he didn't attend practice that night. He told investigators that he spent the night completing homework and relaxing by playing video games.

Mark Staffi
Age: 15
Position: Defense

Background:
This is Mark's second year in high school and first year with the team. Mark is a skilled hockey player. He was asked to try out in his grade 9

Alibi:
Mark has been injured and his immediate playing future is in jeopardy. He claims that he is a victim of

year, but declined as he didn't feel that he would be able to handle the pressure associated with being on the hockey team. He has a quiet personality. He decided to try out this year based on advice from Scott. Mark and Scott are neighbors and even though there is a one year difference between the two, they are very close. When Scott said that he was going to try out for the team, he encouraged Matt to join up. Both players made the team and are now a defensive pair.

bullying and that most of the members of the team were in on it. He said that most people are to blame and can't single out just one individual. He has become withdrawn and reclusive.

Mark will not testify nor will he prepare a Victim Impact Statement.

Wei Shien Gao
Age: 18
Position: Right Wing

Background:
Wei is in his second year with the team. He first made the team when he was in grade 10. He was doing well but got into a few altercations with other team members. As such, he decided to take a year away from hockey and concentrate on school. However, because most of the people he had conflicts with graduated, when the coaching staff asked him to reconsider joining the team, he readily accepted, having missed playing. The coaching staff is hoping that the one year layoff hasn't affected his game.

Alibi:
Wei claimed that he was there when Mark was injured but was scared and did as everyone else, left the arena. When he later found out the injuries were severe he went to the hospital and told Mark's parents what had happened. He claimed that they were just "goofing around" and Mark's injuries were an accident.

Steven Jae Wook
Age: 17
Position: Center

Background:
Steven is a very skilled but emotional player. Many people believe that Steven could be playing on the first line, but for the fact that his emotions land him in the penalty box more often that not. Last year, in only his second year on the team, he had the fifth highest number of points, the third

Alibi:
Steven claims that he was already in the change room when the accident occurred so he didn't personally witness anything. He says that the team often plays pranks which aren't meant to be malicious and are not really planned. He stated

highest number of goals and the second highest number of penalty minutes (only after Paul). His coaches have tried everything to get him to focus more on point production and less on the "other stuff" but to no avail. Ironically, his teachers think that he is one of the most understanding people they have met in class.

that the only reason that he left was because Wei was his ride home. So when Wei said he had to leave, he left with him. He said he didn't really know what happened until later.

Taylor Powell
Age: 17
Position: Defense

Background:
Taylor is one of the most skilled skaters on UCC. He logs some of the highest numbers of minutes on the team. If it's a power play, Taylor's sent on. If it's a penalty kill, Taylor's sent on. This is Taylor's third year on the team but first playing defense. His father requested that Taylor be moved from forward to defense. His father, who is a major contributor to UCC, felt that his son was being underutilized as a forward and wanted the coaching staff to increase his son's playing time (despite already logging some of the highest numbers of minutes on the team). He also believed that scouts may be more interested in a player that "can-do-it-all". The coaching staff made the switch under protest and are on record as saying they "would rather have Taylor remain as a forward and work on that part of his game".

Alibi:
Taylor claims that he left before the incident occurred. He says that he doesn't really participate in team pranks, so the players don't include him in them. He denies knowing anything about the incident.

Brian Moore
Age: 17
Position: Defense

Background:
This is Brian's second year on the team. He is a skilled hockey player but one of the previous coaches is on record as saying that "Brian

Alibi:
Brian states that he didn't know what was going on because he was in the locker room attending to some of

believes he's better than he actually is and does not work as hard as he should". He is quick to accept praise for his accomplishments and just as quick to deflect any criticism. His school work is average, and teachers find "no problems" with him during class time, citing only laziness as an issue. Brian believes that he will definitely be actively recruited in his senior year, and is not stressed about his future plans.

the practice equipment that was left over. He said that once he had finished he walked out as usual. He said that he was surprised that most people had left so quickly but didn't notice anything out of the ordinary.

Lucas Greene
Age: 18
Position: Defense

Background:
Lucas is a fourth year senior with UCC. He's 6'5, 264 lbs with a "booming slap shot". He logs the most number of minutes on the team and was offered the "A" on several occasions but refused. Many of his teammates look to him as a leader on the team and he acts the part. He is quick to encourage his teammates and is very vocal in the dressing room. His teachers describe him as a "pleasant young man". His grades are average, but he works hard to achieve them. Many people have suggested that if he were to improve his grades, he would win the "Canderberry Oishie" trophy; which is awarded to one graduating student that has a high GPA and shows excellence in a sport.

Alibi:
Lucas said that he was frustrated after the practice and just wanted to leave. He said that he didn't acknowledge anyone after practice due to his frustration. He says that because of this, no one let him in on the prank and so he wasn't aware of anything until the following day.

Fitzgerald Stone
Age: 18
Position: Goalie

Background:
This is Fitzgerald's fourth year on the team and second year as the team's starting goalie. He inherited the role last year. He's an unorthodox goalie with a bit of a

Alibi:
Fitz said that he stayed on the ice a little after practice to work on his game, but once most people started to get off, he left. He said that

fiery side. Last year he was the second most penalized goalie in the league. Before attending UCC, Fitzgerald had a very successful run with the Evergreen Hawks Club team. He won a "First Team Rep" award, was on a local "Goalies to Watch" list and was invited to an under 17 development tryout, but never made the team. It was difficult for him to be in a back-up role in his first two years at UCC.

he noticed some teammates got undressed unusually quickly, but didn't think twice about it. He said that it takes goalies a lot longer to get changed because of the extra equipment. Because of this he missed the incident, and just left.

Neal Porter
Age: 16
Position: Goalie

Background:
Neal was the biggest surprise to make the roster. During the selection camp, Neal hoped to make the team as a walk-on. He not only impressed the coaching staff, but he impressed the players as well. Before making the UCC squad, his past teams weren't very successful but were always competitive. He's never been a "number 1" goalie or back up. In fact, on every team that he's played on, he's split time with another goalie. He is a mild mannered young man and very reserved in the locker room.

Alibi:
Neal claims that he left the ice immediately after 11:00pm. He says that he didn't want to stay behind more than he had to, especially since Aiden and Gerome weren't there. He says that his mom picked him up at around 11:20pm, and she has confirmed his statement.

Alistair Little
Age: 32
Position: Head Coach

Background:
Alistair is the new head coach of the UCC hockey program. His highest level of hockey is at the semi-pro level. His career was cut short due to injury. He suffered two major concussions which kept him out of action for the better part of a season and a half. When he was finally given the green light to return, he sustained a knee

No Alibi

injury which prompted him to retire on the advice of his family, doctors and coaches. He stepped away from hockey for a few years until accepting a coaching position with a struggling bantam club team. The team had immediate success under his guidance. The reversal of fortune for the team landed Alistair a "Coach of the Year" award. UCC took notice, and with their old coach retiring, offered Alistair the head coaching position.

Phillip McCoy
Age: 46
Position:
Assistant Coach

Background:
Phillip is the returning assistant coach for UCC. He's been with the team for six years. Although he was passed over for the head coaching position he does not seem bitter about it. It was widely speculated that if he were offered the position he would have turned it down anyway, and so UCC went to Alistair with their offer. After Alistair accepted the position however, he contacted Phillip and asked him to remain with the team to help maintain stability while the transition of head coaches transpired. Phillip agreed. Phillip has never played hockey at a high level but has a wealth of hockey knowledge.

No Alibi

Anthony Garrett
Age: 33
Position:
Assistant Coach

Background:
Anthony was the assistant coach with Alistair on the bantam club team. When Alistair was asked to become the coach he negotiated a "Phys-Ed" teaching position as

No Alibi

well as assistant coach position for Anthony. Anthony played semi-pro for several years but became disillusioned regarding his prospects of playing anything higher. He grew tired of seeing younger players join the team and then move up to the bigger clubs instead of him and decided to retire from the game. He took a job as an instructor at a rink. There, he met Alistair who offered him his original assistant coaching position. From then on the two have worked together.

The Upper Crescent College Hockey Hazing Trial
Prosecution vs. Defense

K.J. Sukhu

Evidence
The evidence is really all you have to go on

Really make sense of the evidence. There are many stories buried in the data. Even things that seem inconsequential may be vital to either defending or prosecuting these young men. Details can make or break your case.

The Evidence Package Includes

Item 1.	List of Teams that Currently Play in the UIHA
Item 2.	Upper Crescent College Schedule
Item 3.	Player Statistics
Item 4.	Conference Statistics for Teams Other than UCC
Item 5	Team Depth Chart
Item 6.	Records of Booked Ice Time at Upper Ice Center
Item 7.	The Upper Crescent College Hockey Team Contract
Item 8.	Band Events – Home Games Scheduled for Upper Crescent College
Item 9.	Official Police Report
Item 10.	Doctor Physicals: Upper Cresent College Players
Item 11.	Two Movie Stubs Provided by Elisabeth Leucete
Item 12.	Receipt Provided by Michael, Austin and Paul
Item 13.	Letter from Alistair Little to the Athletic Council
Item 14.	Phone Records
Item 15.	List of Phone Numbers

The Upper Crescent College Hockey Hazing Trial
Prosecution vs. Defense

K.J. Sukhu

Evidence: Item 1
List of Teams that Currently Play in the UIHA

Non Relegated Teams in the League	
Conference A	**Conference B**
Upper Crescent College (UCC)	Cardinal James Academy
Highland Bishop Academy (HBA)	Parkdale Day School
David & Mary Preparatory School (D&MP)	St. Gabriel Schools
Greenwich "Golden Archers" College	Matriarch Benzenia Arts Academy
Browning Academy	Holy Trinity Cross Schools
Sovereign Family of Schools	Harbinger Preparatory School
Sandalphon Academy	Guardian Pilgrimage International School
Covenant of the Blessed Spirit	Infinite Light Preparatory School

The Upper Crescent College Hockey Hazing Trial
Prosecution vs. Defense

K.J. Sukhu

Evidence: Item 2
Upper Crescent College Schedule

MM/DD	Home			Away
10/02	Upper Crescent College	1	3	Greenwich College
10/04	Upper Crescent College	3	5	Browning Academy
10/07	Browning Academy	5	2	Upper Crescent College
10/10	Sovereign FoS	1	6	Upper Crescent College
10/15	Upper Crescent College	1	4	Sandalphon Academy
10/18	Holy Trinity Cross School	6	5	Upper Crescent College
10/23	St. Gabriel Schools	0	4	Upper Crescent College
10/24	Upper Crescent College	3	4	St. Gabriel Schools
10/29*	Upper Crescent College	3	4	Covenant of the Blessed Spirit
10/31	Parkdale Day School	5	3	Upper Crescent College
11/02	Upper Crescent College	2	4	Harbinger Preparatory School
11/05	Upper Crescent College	6	2	Matriarch Benzenia Arts Acdmy
11/07	Upper Crescent College	5	1	Cardinal James Academy
11/11*	David & Mary Preparatory	5	4	Upper Crescent College
11/14	Guardian Pilgrimage	3	6	Upper Crescent College
11/17	Upper Crescent College	1	7	Highland Bishop Academy
11/20	Infinite Light Preparatory	3	5	Upper Crescent College
11/23	Upper Crescent College	2	4	David & Mary Preparatory
11/26	Upper Crescent College	5	1	Sovereign FoS
11/30	Greenwich College	3	2	Upper Crescent College
12/03	Covenant of Blessed Spirit	4	3	Upper Crescent College
12/06	Sandalphon Academy	1	4	Upper Crescent College
12/09	Upper Crescent College	5	6	Parkdale Day School
12/11	Harbinger Preparatory	5	3	Upper Crescent College
12/15	Upper Crescent College	5	3	Holy Trinity Cross
12/19*	Cardinal James Academy	3	2	Upper Crescent College
12/20	Matriarch Benzenia Arts	2	6	Upper Crescent College
12/22	Highland Bishop Academy	6	4	Upper Crescent College
12/27	Upper Crescent College	4	5	Infinite Light Preparatory
12/29*	Upper Crescent College	2	3	Guardian Pilgrimage
01/04	Upper Crescent College	2	5	Harbinger Preparatory School
01/07	Harbinger Preparatory	5	3	Upper Crescent College
01/09	David & Mary Preparatory	6	3	Upper Crescent College
01/13	Upper Crescent College	4	0	St. Gabriel Schools
01/16	Holy Trinity Cross	5	1	Upper Crescent College

The Upper Crescent College Hockey Hazing Trial K.J. Sukhu
Prosecution vs. Defense

01/20	Upper Crescent College	5	2	Holy Trinity Cross
01/23	Cardinal James Academy	1	4	Upper Crescent College
01/27	Infinite Light Preparatory	6	2	Upper Crescent College
01/30	Upper Crescent College	5	2	Matriarch Benzenia Arts
02/04*	Guardian Pilgrimage	4	3	Upper Crescent College
02/07	Upper Crescent College	2	5	Parkdale Day School
02/11	Upper Crescent College	4	2	Sandalphon Academy
02/14	Covenant of Blessed Spirit	5	3	Upper Crescent College
02/18	Greenwich College	2	4	Upper Crescent College
02/23	Browning Academy	7	3	Upper Crescent College
02/28	Sovereign FoS	1	5	Upper Crescent College
03/04	Upper Crescent College	2	4	Sovereign FoS
48: TBD	Sandalphon Academy			Upper Crescent College
49: TBD	Upper Crescent College			Browning Academy
50: TBD	Highland Bishop Academy			Upper Crescent College
51: TBD	Upper Crescent College			Highland Bishop Academy
52: TBD	Parkdale Day School			Upper Crescent College
53: TBD	Upper Crescent College			David & Mary Preparatory
54: TBD	Upper Crescent College			Greenwich College
55: TBD	Upper Crescent College			Covenant of the Blessed Spirit
56: TBD	St. Gabriel Schools			Upper Crescent College
57: TBD	Matriarch Benzenia Arts			Upper Crescent College
58: TBD	Upper Crescent College			Guardian Pilgrimage
59: TBD	Upper Crescent College			Cardinal James Academy
60: TBD	Upper Crescent College			Infinite Light Preparatory

* Indicates games that went into overtime/shootout

The Upper Crescent College Hockey Hazing Trial
Prosecution vs. Defense

K.J. Sukhu

Evidence: Item 3
Player Statistics

#		Player	GP	G	A	P	+/-	PIM	PP	SH	GW	S	S%
44	C	Jeff Fordice	47	13	26	39	+9	14	3	0	0	80	16.2
16	LW	Anthony Campelli	40	11	19	30	+2	22	2	0	0	76	14.5
14	C	Steven Jae Wook	47	17	20	37	-9	36	3	0	0	67	25.3
08	D	Mark Staffi	47	2	18	20	-6	4	0	0	0	36	5.5
28	RW	Paul Frasier	47	3	23	25	0	89	0	0	0	67	4.5
03	D	Scott McAferdy	47	6	21	27	-7	0	1	0	0	44	13.6
17	LW	Gerome Thompson	47	33	21	54	+6	6	8	3	3	141	23.4
11	LW	Matt Defrancesco	47	2	5	7	-4	2	0	0	0	67	2.9
24	RW	Wei Shien Gao	45	11	19	30	-3	4	1	0	0	61	18
09	C	Austin Rodriguez	47	19	28	47	0	2	3	1	2	132	14.4
02	D	Brian Moore	47	5	16	21	-7	11	1	0	0	48	10.4
12	D	Taylor Powell	47	12	31	43	-3	3	5	1	0	124	9.6
04	D	Michael Bishop	47	2	11	13	-9	10	0	0	0	46	4.3
88	D	Lucas Greene	47	7	25	32	-4	24	4	0	0	89	7.8
07	RW	Aiden Waters	47	21	19	40	+4	2	4	1	4	154	13.6

#		Player	GPI	Min	P	W	L	OT	SH	SO	SV%	PIM
33	G	Fitzgerald Stone	X	1003	2	10	17	1		0	.87	4
29	G	Neal Porter	X	831	0	7	8	4		2	.94	0

IMPORTANT: This report contains proprietary and original material. Accordingly, this document may not be copied or released to third parties without consent.

The Upper Crescent College Hockey Hazing Trial
Prosecution vs. Defense

Evidence: Item 4
Conference Statistics for all teams other than UCC
(UCC had a stat tracker for all teams other than themselves)

Conference A				
Team	Wins	Losses	OTL	Points
Browning Academy	34	7	6	74
David & Mary Preparatory School	32	8	7	71
Highland Bishop Academy	28	6	13	69
Greenwich College	29	16	2	60
Covenant of Blessed Spirit	22	17	8	52
Sovereign Family of Schools	17	27	3	37
Sandalphon Academy	15	29	3	33
Conference B				
Team	Wins	Losses	OTL	Points
Infinite Light Preparatory	33	8	6	72
Parkdale Day School	32	6	8	72
Harbinger Preparatory School	32	11	4	68
Matriarch Benzenia Arts Academy	26	18	3	55
Guardian Pilgrimage International School	25	21	1	51
St. Gabriel Schools	23	19	5	51
Holy Trinity Cross Schools	19	21	7	45
Cardinal James Academy	18	24	5	41

The Upper Crescent College Hockey Hazing Trial
Prosecution vs. Defense

K.J. Sukhu

Evidence: Item 5
Team Depth Chart

Team Depth Chart

LW	C	RW
Anthony Campelli (A)	Jeff Fordice (C)	Paul Frasier
Gerome Thompson	Austin Rodriguez (A)	Aiden Waters
Matt Defrancesco	Steven Jae Wook	Wei Shien Gao

LD	RD
Taylor Powell	Lucas Greene
Brian Moore	Michael Bishop
Mark Staffi	Scott Mcferdy

G
Fitzgerald Stone
Neal Porter

Post Selection Camp, Pre First Game

The Upper Crescent College Hockey Hazing Trial
Prosecution vs. Defense

K.J. Sukhu

Evidence: Item 6
Records of Booked Ice Time at Upper Ice Center

The Upper Ice Centre – "The Experience is Top Notch" Official Rink of the Upper Crescent College Hockey Team Booking Receipts Provided for UCC Members					
Date (MM/DD)	Price	Payment	Purchaser	Time Allotted	Rink
09/01	$220.00	Cash	Mr. J. Fordice	10:00pm – 11:00pm	1
09/04	$220.00	Credit Card	Mrs. J. Campelli	10:00pm – 11:00pm	1
09/08	$220.00	Credit Card	Mrs. F. Rodriguez	10:00pm – 11:00pm	1
09/11	$220.00	Cash	Mr. J. Fordice	10:00pm – 11:00pm	1
09/15	$220.00	Credit Card	Mr. A. Campelli	10:00pm – 11:00pm	1
09/22	$220.00	Credit Card	Mrs. F. Rodriguez	10:00pm – 11:00pm	1
09/27	$220.00	Credit Card	Mr. J. Fordice	10:00pm – 11:00pm	1
10/05	$220.00	Credit Card	Mr. P. Defrancesco	10:00pm – 11:00pm	1
10/12	$185.00	Credit Card	Mrs. S. Waters	10:00pm – 11:00pm	2
10/20	$220.00	Credit Card	Mrs. D. McAferdy	10:00pm – 11:00pm	1
10/27	$220.00	Credit Card	Mr. N. Porter	10:00pm – 11:00pm	1
11/04	$220.00	Credit Card	Mrs. L. Staffi	10:00pm – 11:00pm	1
11/18	$160.00	Cash	Mr. G. Thompson	10:00pm – 11:00pm	3
11/24	$220.00	Credit Card	Mr. P. Defrancesco	10:00pm – 11:00pm	1
12/01	$185.00	Credit Card	Mrs. D. McAferdy	10:00pm – 11:00pm	2
12/08	$185.00	Credit Card	Mr. J. Staffi	10:00pm – 11:00pm	2
12/16	$185.00	Credit Card	Mr. Porter	10:00pm – 11:00pm	2
12/25	$220.00	Credit Card	Mr. W. Gao	10:00pm – 11:00pm	1
01/05	$220.00	Credit Card	Mr. L. Greene	10:00pm – 11:00pm	1
01/21	$220.00	Credit Card	Mr. P. Defrancesco	10:00pm – 11:00pm	1
02/08	$220.00	Cash	Mr. J. Fordice	10:00pm – 11:00pm	1
02/21	$220.00	Credit Card	Mrs. J. Campelli	10:00pm – 11:00pm	1
03/05 ***	$220.00	Cash	Mr. A. Rodriguez	10:00pm – 11:00pm	1

Evidence: Item 7

The Upper Crescent College Hockey Team Contract

The Upper Crescent College Hockey Team Contract

It is a tremendous honor to accept a position with UCC hockey. I understand that playing within a team will have ups and downs. I will strive to be a humble winner and be gracious in defeat. The schedule I am undertaking is daunting. However, it is not an excuse for low marks. Education will always put me further in life than anything else. I will complete all assignments, homework, tests and quizzes for which I am responsible. I will never use hockey as an excuse for late or missed assignments. If my grades ever fall below an average of 60% I will be placed on academic probation and will miss all games and practices until my marks improve.

I will use the knowledge of my coaches and teachers to help better myself as a player and person. I will work to improve the reputation of UCC, as members of UCC work hard to uplift me. My time on the team will help to prepare me to handle obstacles later in life and so I will use this experience as a learning opportunity. I acknowledge that I am part of a team, I am not above the team and my attitude and work ethic will reflect this. I will take responsibility for my actions on and off the ice.

Any member that puts on the UCC jersey has earned it. It is not up to me to agree with the selection choices but it is up to me to work together to achieve the best possible outcome for the team. I'm ready for the challenge that awaits me. It is an experience that I will reflect on going forward.

I _____, have read through the contract in its entirety with my guardians _____ & _____. I acknowledge that failure to abide by the guidelines stated above will result in my termination from the team.

_____ _____
Student's Signature *Date*

_____ _____ _____
Guardian's Signature 1 *Guardians's Signature 2* *Date*

The Upper Crescent College Hockey Hazing Trial
Prosecution vs. Defense

Evidence: Item 8

Band Events – Home Games Scheduled for Upper Crescent College

Band Events – Home Games Scheduled for Upper Crescent College *		
Date (MM/DD)	**Event**	**Uniform**
09/23	UCC Varsity Hockey Team Acknowledgment Ceremony	Green
10/02	UCC vs. Greenwich "Golden Archers" College	Green
10/04	UCC vs. Browning Academy	Green
10/15	UCC vs. Sandalphon Academy	Green
10/24	UCC vs. St. Gabriel Schools	Green
10/29	UCC vs. Covenant of the Blessed Spirit	Green
11/02	UCC vs. Harbinger Preparatory School	Green
11/07	UCC vs. Cardinal James Academy	Green
11/17	UCC vs. Highland Bishop Academy	Green
11/23	UCC vs. David & Mary Preparatory School	Green
12/09	UCC vs. Parkdale Day School	Green
TBD	TBD	TBD
TBD	TBD	TBD
TBD	TBD	TBD
TBD	TBD	TBD
TBD	TBD	TBD
TBD	TBD	TBD

* Revised Schedule – Modified Version from Original

The Upper Crescent College Hockey Hazing Trial K.J. Sukhu
Prosecution vs. Defense

Evidence: Item 9
Official Police Report

Case Number: 20XX-00053450

Reporting Officer:
James Hadfield

Date of Report:
March 5th 20XX

At approximately 23:45, 5 March 20XX, Officers, EMS and Fire were dispatched to 46 Venture Way Drive for a male unconscious on the ice. EMS workers F. Smyth and T. Brown were attending a white male who was wearing skates and shorts. The male was later identified as Mark Staffi.

Scott McAferdy, who contacted 911, reported that he and his friend Mark Staffi entered *The Upper Ice Centre* at 21:30 hours to play hockey with his high school team. Mr. McAferdy, who was dressed in a wet, white t-shirt and shorts, explained that the practice concluded at around 23:00, however several teammates remained behind. Mr. McAferdy identified the other teammates as a Mr. Jeff Fordice, Mr. Anthony Campelli, Mr. Steven Jae Wook, Mr. Paul Frasier, Mr. Matt Defrancesco, Mr. Wei Shien Gao, Mr. Austin Rodriguez, Mr. Brian Moore, Mr. Taylor Powell, Mr. Fitzgerald Stone, Mr. Neal Porter, Mr. Michael Bishop, and a Mr. Lucas Greene.

Mr. McAferdy estimated that at 23:20 Mark and Scott engaged in a "competition" in which the two "attempted to skate with the puck from one end of the rink to the next, blindfolded". Mr. McAferdy reported hearing a loud "gasp" from the other players during the competition. He called out to see what the commotion was about and received no reply. When he finally removed his blindfold a few minutes later, he witnessed Mr. Staffi motionless on the ice. He then went to dressing room "#6" to retrieve his cell phone and call 9-1-1.

I provided Mr. McAferdy with Precinct 71's card and informed him that there would be a follow up to the investigation. He was then released into the care of his parents who had arrived on the scene.

Evidence: Item 10

Doctor Physicals: Upper Cresent College Player

	10/01/20XX		11/29/20XX		02/03/20XX		Notes
	Systolic Range	Diastolic Range	Systolic Range	Diastolic Range	Systolic Range	Diastolic Range	
Mr. Fordice	127	84	128	84	130	86	
Mr. Campelli	120	80	120	80	120	80	
Mr. Wook	119	80	120	82	120	80	
Mr. Staffi	111	77	114	78	113	77	
Mr. Frasier	127	84	124	84	128	84	
Mr. McAferdy	109	75	112	78	112	78	
Mr. Thompson	109	75	109	75	110	77	
Mr. Defrancesco	109	75	111	78	112	77	
Mr. Gao	121	80	120	80	120	80	
Mr. Rodriguez	121	82	121	83	121	81	
Mr. Moore	120	82	121	82	121	83	
Mr. Powell	119	80	120	82	120	80	
Mr. Stone	105	73	108	75	112	77	
Mr. Porter	109	73	111	75	112	77	
Mr. Bishop	122	82	122	82	122	83	
Mr. Greene	127	84	128	84	128	86	
Mr. Waters	117	75	120	82	120	80	

The Upper Crescent College Hockey Hazing Trial
Prosecution vs. Defense

K.J. Sukhu

Evidence: Item 11
Two Movie Stubs Provided by Elisabeth Leucete

The Upper Crescent College Hockey Hazing Trial
Prosecution vs. Defense

Evidence: Item 12
Receipt Provided by Michael, Austin and Paul

```
        "A-OK" Oak Burgers
  7 Alex              SU 03
  ---------------------------------
   ORDR 85           3/6  00:23am


        3 Ok DB         6.60
        3 Fries         3.33
        2 water         4.50

        Subtotal       14.43
        Tax             2.03
        Payment        20.00
        Change Due      3.54


   Thanks for eating at "A-OK"
   Oak Burgers.
   Our burgers are great inside
   and out!
```

Evidence: Item 13

Letter from Alistair Little to the Athletic Council

To: The Attention of the UCC Athletic Council,

Regarding the $8,000 and $4,000 earmarked for the Varsity team and Junior Team respectively, I wish to request a change in the funding formula. Based on the ongoing season, and taking into consideration the ongoing success and tradition of UCC, I feel that the $8,000 for the varsity team would be better spent on the junior team, while the varsity team can manage with the $4,000. The additional funds to the junior team will be better spent on player development with a focus on player strengthening, increased ice time and team building activities. As most of the seniors are leaving this year, the coaching staff believes that this will strengthen the hockey program for years to come.

Kind Regards,

Alistair Little

The Upper Crescent College Hockey Hazing Trial
Prosecution vs. Defense

K.J. Sukhu

Evidence: Item 14
Phone Records

XX/XX/XXXX

Billed Usage

"Whoa" Phone Company

MACRO/CELL
Billed Usage

Run Date: 03/05/XX & 03/06/XX
Run Time: N/A
Accoun: N/A ~ accounts subpoenaed and aggregated for court use

AWS   White Oak Mountain

Mobile	Rate Plan Description	Called Loc	Called Phone	Date	Time (Standard)	Duration
(555)xxx-4671	Roamer rate plan	White Oak Mtn.	(555)xxx-3942	03/05/XX	7:54 pm	2 min
(555)xxx-2142	Roamer rate plan	White Oak Mtn.	(555)xxx-2180	03/05/XX	7:56 pm	1 min
(555)xxx-2180	Roamer rate plan	White Oak Mtn.	(555)xxx-3178	03/05/XX	7:58 pm	2 min
(555)xxx-2142	Roamer rate plan	White Oak Mtn.	(555)xxx-3178	03/05/XX	7:58 pm	0 min
(555)xxx-2142	Roamer rate plan	White Oak Mtn.	(555)xxx-3178	03/05/XX	8:03 pm	3 min
(555)xxx-3124	Roamer rate plan	White Oak Mtn.	(555)xxx-2142	03/05/XX	8:10 pm	2 min
(555)xxx-4671	Roamer rate plan	White Oak Mtn.	(555)xxx-3942	03/05/XX	8:14 pm	2 min
(555)xxx-3192	Roamer rate plan	White Oak Mtn.	(555)xxx-3942	03/05/XX	8:26 pm	2 min
(555)xxx-2142	Roamer rate plan	White Oak Mtn.	(555)xxx-4671	03/05/XX	8:26 pm	2 min
(555)xxx-7160	Roamer rate plan	White Oak Mtn.	(555)xxx-1467	03/05/XX	8:30 pm	2 min
(555)xxx-7160	Roamer rate plan	White Oak Mtn.	(555)xxx-2170	03/05/XX	8:42 pm	2 min
(555)xxx-7160	Roamer rate plan	White Oak Mtn.	(555)xxx-5691	03/05/XX	8:45 pm	2 min
(555)xxx-5731	Roamer rate plan	White Oak Mtn.	(555)xxx-2982	03/05/XX	8:50 pm	2 min
(555)xxx-5731	Roamer rate plan	White Oak Mtn.	(555)xxx-3235	03/05/XX	8:53 pm	2 min
(555)xxx-3176	Roamer rate plan	White Oak Mtn.	(555)xxx-5192	03/05/XX	8:54 pm	2 min
(555)xxx-3176	Roamer rate plan	White Oak Mtn.	(555)xxx-3192	03/05/XX	8:57 pm	1 min

IMPORTANT: This report contains proprietary and original material. Accordingly, this document may not be copied or released to third parties without consent.

The Upper Crescent College Hockey Hazing Trial
Prosecution vs. Defense

K.J. Sukhu

(555)xxx-3176	Roamer rate plan	White Oak Mtn.	(555)xxx-3178	03/05/XX	8:59 pm	2 min
(555)xxx-2142	Roamer rate plan	White Oak Mtn.	(555)xxx-4671	03/05/XX	9:03 pm	1 min
(555)xxx-5731	Roamer rate plan	White Oak Mtn.	(555)xxx-2982	03/05/XX	9:15 pm	2 min
(555)xxx-5192	Roamer rate plan	White Oak Mtn.	(555)xxx-2170	03/05/XX	9:30 pm	3 min
(555)xxx-3192	Roamer rate plan	White Oak Mtn.	(555)xxx-3942	03/05/XX	9:33 pm	1 min
(555)xxx-5731	Roamer rate plan	White Oak Mtn.	(555)xxx-2982	03/05/XX	9:35 pm	1 min
(555)xxx-5731	Roamer rate plan	White Oak Mtn.	(555)xxx-3235	03/05/XX	9:37 pm	1 min
(555)xxx-5731	Roamer rate plan	White Oak Mtn.	(555)xxx-3235	03/05/XX	9:42 pm	1 min
(555)xxx-3235	Roamer rate plan	White Oak Mtn.	(555)xxx-3178	03/05/XX	9:55 pm	1 min
(555)xxx-2170	Roamer rate plan	White Oak Mtn.	(555)xxx-5192	03/05/XX	10:04 pm	0 min
(555)xxx-5192	Roamer rate plan	White Oak Mtn.	(555)xxx-2170	03/05/XX	11:21 pm	1 min
(555)xxx-3942	Roamer rate plan	White Oak Mtn.	(555)xxx-5674	03/05/XX	11:41 pm	3min
(555)xxx-3942	Roamer rate plan	White Oak Mtn.	911	03/05/XX	11:44 pm	5 min
(555)xxx-3178	Roamer rate plan	White Oak Mtn.	(555)xxx-1998	03/05/XX	11:48 pm	3 min
(555)xxx-4671	Roamer rate plan	White Oak Mtn.	(555)xxx-9087	03/05/XX	11:50 pm	2 min
(555)xxx-3178	Roamer rate plan	White Oak Mtn.	(555)xxx-2142	03/05/XX	11:53 pm	2 min
(555)xxx-7160	Roamer rate plan	White Oak Mtn.	(555)xxx-2170	03/05/XX	11:56 pm	8 min
(555)xxx-2180	Roamer rate plan	White Oak Mtn.	(555)xxx-3178	03/05/XX	11:56 pm	1 min
(555)xxx-2142	Roamer rate plan	White Oak Mtn.	(555)xxx-2982	03/05/XX	11:57 pm	2 min
(555)xxx-1998	Roamer rate plan	White Oak Mtn.	(555)xxx-3178	03/05/XX	11:58 pm	3 min
(555)xxx-2170	Roamer rate plan	White Oak Mtn.	(555)xxx-3192	03/06/XX	12:06 am	0 min
(555)xxx-2170	Roamer rate plan	White Oak Mtn.	(555)xxx-3942	03/06/XX	12:07 am	0 min
(555)xxx-2170	Roamer rate plan	White Oak Mtn.	(555)xxx-5192	03/06/XX	12:07 am	8 min
(555)xxx-3124	Roamer rate plan	White Oak Mtn.	(555)xxx-2142	03/06/XX	12:07 am	2 min

IMPORTANT: This report contains proprietary and original material. Accordingly, this document may not be copied or released to third parties without consent.

Evidence: Item 15
List of Phone Numbers

Name	Phone Number
Jeff Fordice	(555)xxx-3178
Anthony Campelli	(555)xxx-2142
Steven Jae Wook	(555)xxx-5691
Mark Staffi	(555)xxx-3192
Paul Frasier	(555)xxx-5731
Scott McAferdy	(555)xxx-3942
Gerome Thompson	(555)xxx-2170
Matt Defrancesco	(555)xxx-4671
Wei Shien Gao	(555)xxx-7160
Austin Rodriguez	(555)xxx-3235
Brian Moore	(555)xxx-2180
Taylor Powell	(555)xxx-6220
Fitzgerald Stone	(555)xxx-3124
Neal Porter	(555)xxx-3176
Michael Bishop	(555)xxx-2982
Lucas Greene	(555)xxx-4176
Aiden Waters	(555)xxx-5192
Elizabeth	(555)xxx-1998
Matt's Parents	(555)xxx-9087
Scott's Parents	(555)xxx-5674
Wei's Girlfriend	(555)xxx-1467

Official Statements Taken by Investigators
Some statements that may or may not aid your investigation

The following information was taken from police interviews. All statements can be used in court.

Old Guy at the Rink	"Oh yeah, after any official UCC practice I always let the kids just shoot around for a bit. The ice was never booked at that time, and the kids are good. Plus, the kids regularly booked the ice like almost once a week anyway, so I'm not going to chase them out of here."
Official Press Release for the Convener of the UIHA	"After the hazing situation came to light we were quick to temporarily halt the season. We are currently working with UCC and the authorities to see whether it is best to continue with the season as per usual, or if we should exclude UCC and continue the schedule for the rest of the season. We will have an answer for you as soon as the authorities are finished with their investigation."
Grade 11 Student (Identity Withheld)	"Yeah, the hockey team's jackets are nicer than the basketball and football jackets. It's kind of messed up that only half the team was allowed to wear them the first week though. I guess that's just how it happened to work out this year. Seemed to cause some tension earlier in the season."
Geography Teacher	"The kids tell me that Steven gets a lot of penalties but I can't believe that…in my class he's one of the calmest, coolest, most level-headed students I've ever taught."
Math Teacher	"I can't stand teaching most of the athletes at this school. For the most part the hockey team isn't so bad. But that's my experience. Diane had a run in with a student and I'm guessing she would have a different take."
Alistair	"A lot of traditions can be detrimental to a team. One in particular is the 'practices' that the guys run on their own. Without the right leadership it can undo the great work that was done."

The Upper Crescent College Hockey Hazing Trial
Prosecution vs. Defense

Grade 12 Student (Identity Withheld)	"I hate the jocks in this school. They think that they can get away with anything… look at Gerome. The guy caused a huge scene… and what happened to him… a couple hours of raking leaves. He should be suspended. That kind of stuff shouldn't be tolerated at UCC."
Mrs. Diane Lane	"If a student is failing a course then I will definitely take them out of athletics. In the past I found the coaches fought me on it, but the coaching staff this year has been really supportive of my decision, so that was great."
Anthony Garrett	"Gerome is a great hockey talent. He's got great skills; his attitude is top-notch; always shows up early for every practice and is one of the hardest working players. He's a great kid."
Upper Ice Centre Manager	"Our video camera system was offline during the time the 'incident' occured. In fact our cameras hadn't been running for a week prior to that. We followed all regulations and notified authorities and were assured we would not be liable. We were told we may still conduct business as usual. Although not responsible, we do feel for the families of everyone in this situation, especially the young male that was hurt."
Athletic Director	"The letter that Mr. Little wrote was leaked by an unknown source, probably a week before the incident."
Tutor	"There are private tutors, about three of us, who travel with the team to ensure school work is being taken care of."
Band Director	"I gave the revised schedule to the authorities. We revised it a couple times during the season. But the version I gave the authorities is the most up-to-date version yet."
Tutor	"Practices were getting less frequent because it was taking a toll on everyone."

The Phases of the Trial
This is a breakdown of how the trial will proceed

Read the phases of trial. Understanding how the trial will proceed will be vital in the development of your strategy.

Phase 1: Going Through the Evidence and Setting the Charges
- A List of Possible Charges
- Punishments
- How Do I Put a Charge Together?

Phase 2: The Bail Hearing
- Bail Condition Examples
- Bail Conditions Proposal

Phase 3: Selecting People Who Will Testify

Phase 4: The Trial Can Now Begin

Phase 5: The Conclusion

The Upper Crescent College Hockey Hazing Trial
Prosecution vs. Defense

K.J. Sukhu

Phase 1
Going through the evidence and setting the charges

After going through the evidence and taking a position (either Prosecution or Defense) you will start preparing your case.

PROSECUTION	DEFENSE
- Look through all of the available information and evidence - Write down any questions you wish to ask the students during the trial - Lay charges on specific characters	- Look through all of the available information and evidence - Write down any questions you wish to ask the students during the trial - Look through the Prosecution's charges
- Hand in a list of your charges to your instructor and to the Defense	- Nothing to hand in

The Prosecution's Task:
As the prosecution, you will go through the evidence (very carefully) and lay charges on certain characters.

* Note: Take time to go through the evidence. Laying charges that shouldn't be laid can destroy your whole case (this decision should not be made lightly).

The Prosecution should also determine what type of charges should be laid see "List of Possible Charges". The strategy you use will have repercussions down the line. In addition to choosing which charges to lay, you will decide what "class" the charge will be.

Throughout the trial you will also attempt to plead your case for either consecutive or concurrent charges.

Some things to consider:
- Will everyone have the same charges?
- Will some characters have unique charges?
- Will some characters not be charged at all?

A List of Possible Charges

Note: You may research other possible charges not listed below

Accessory to a Crime — Aiding in a crime or withholding information while a crime takes place is a crime in itself.

Aiding and Abetting — Helping another person carry out a crime even if you are not directly involved in a crime is a criminal act.

Assault — Assault usually involves actual physical contact, but one may be charged with assault without actually touching another if one's actions resulted in bodily harm of another.

Child Abuse — Any act that harms a child. This can also include failure to act to protect a child.

Conspiracy — If two or more parties plot to commit a crime and act towards carrying out the plan, charges may be laid.

Harassment — Any behavior that is purposely used to torment, annoy and upset an individual may be considered harassment.

Hate Crimes — Any crime carried out on the basis of race, ethnicity, national origin, religion, disability, or sexuality.

Perjury — Anyone who takes the stand but lies knowingly under oath.

Criminal Mischief — Anyone who damages property with criminal intent.

Child Endangerment — Abuse of a child either in a physical, emotional or sexual manner.

Contributing to the Delinquency of a Minor — Any action taken by an adult that results in immoral behavior.

Menacing — Attempting to place someone in fear of physical injury or death by displaying a weapon.

Other Possible Charges to Research?			
Fleeing the Scene	Intimidation of a Witness	Reckless Endangerment	Threats
Obstruction	Risk Causing a Catastrophe	Unlawful Restraint	Unlawful Assembly

*Note: Not all of these charges may be relevant to the case. Be careful of which charges you lay.

The Upper Crescent College Hockey Hazing Trial
Prosecution vs. Defense

K.J. Sukhu

Punishments
Different classes of punishments

*Note: Different jurisdictions weigh felonies and misdemeanors differently. In this case we will only consider these fabricated misdemeanor and felony charges.

Misdemeanor Charge
A misdemeanor carries a minimum sentence of one day and a maximum sentence of one year of imprisonment, with a mandatory three month period of probation. Additional fines start at $1.00 and go up a maximum of $10,000.

Felony Charges

Class 5 Felony	Carries a minimum sentence of thirty days and a maximum sentence of two years of imprisonment, with a mandatory six month period of probation.
Class 4 Felony	Carries a minimum sentence of six months and a maximum sentence of four years imprisonment, with a mandatory one year period of probation (with a possibility of up to an additional year).
Class 3 Felony	Carries a minimum sentence of one year of imprisonment and a maximum of eight years of imprisonment, with a mandatory one year period of probation (with a possibility of up to two additional years).

Class 2 Felony	Carries a minimum sentence of three years of imprisonment and a maximum sentence of fifteen years of imprisonment, with a mandatory two year period of probation (with a possibility of up to two additional years).
Class 1 Felony	Carries a minimum sentence of five years of imprisonment and a maximum sentence of twenty five years of imprisonment, with a mandatory three year period of probation (with a possibility of up to three additional years).

*Note: You must be realistic when deciding on what class felony you would like to attach to the charge. For example, for this case, if you were to attach a Class 1 Felony to a charge, the case will definitely be thrown out and the defense would be successful. Choose wisely.

IMPORTANT: This report contains proprietary and original material. Accordingly, this document may not be copied or released to third parties without consent.

The Upper Crescent College Hockey Hazing Trial
Prosecution vs. Defense

K.J. Sukhu

How Do I Put a Charge Together?
You will hand in a list of charges to your instructor as well as to the defense team.

Example of Putting a Charge Together:
Let's say that after going through the evidence you decide that you want to charge Assistant Coach Phillip McCoy with the following charges:
1. Hate Crime
2. Menacing
3. Assault

You feel that you have a fairly weak case on the Hate Crime charge so you decide that a misdemeanor charge is the best strategy.

For the Menacing charge, you feel confident in your case and evidence so you decide you will try and go after a Class 5 Felony charge.

However, on the Assault charge you feel that your case is pretty much "in the bag" and you feel that you can pursue a Class 4 Felony charge.

You will then simply fill in the chart, provided on the next page, as demonstrated below. You will find (but are not limited to) a list of charges and punishments on the previous pages.

Person	Charge	Type of Charge (Punishment)
Phillip McCoy	- Hate Crimes - Menacing - Assault	- Misdemeanor - Class 5 Felony - Class 4 Felony

Remember, even if you have a great case, if the punishment doesn't fit the crime you will lose your case.

A Misdemeanor Charge	→	Poses a small challenge to obtain.
A Class 5 Felony Charge	→	Poses some challenge to obtain.
A Class 4 Felony Charge	→	Will be very challenging to obtain.
A Class 3 Felony Charge	→	Will be almost impossible to obtain and may result in your defeat.
A Class 1 or 2 Felony Charge	→	Will automatically be thrown out.

IMPORTANT: This report contains proprietary and original material. Accordingly, this document may not be copied or released to third parties without consent.

The Upper Crescent College Hockey Hazing Trial
Prosecution vs. Defense

K.J. Sukhu

Person	Charge	Type of Charge (Punishment)
Jeff Fordice		
Anthony Campelli		
Steven Jae Wook		
Mark Staffi		
Paul Frasier		
Scott McAferdy		
Gerome Thompson		
Matt Defrancesco		
Wei Shien Gao		
Austin Rodriguez		

The Upper Crescent College Hockey Hazing Trial
Prosecution vs. Defense

K.J. Sukhu

Brian Moore		
Taylor Powell		
Fitzgerald Stone		
Neal Porter		
Michael Bishop		
Lucas Greene		
Aiden Waters		
Anthony Garrett		
Alistair Little		
Phillip McCoy		

The Upper Crescent College Hockey Hazing Trial
Prosecution vs. Defense

Defense:
When the Prosecution unveils their charges you will be tasked with refuting these charges. Go through the evidence, analyze the Prosecution's claims and come up with a counter. Your goal is to have all charges dropped.

- Use your time wisely to go through all the evidence (this is essential).
- While going through your evidence, figure out which characters you want on the witness stands and possible questions you would ask them.
- When the Prosecution presents the charges, you will only have a limited amount of time to come up with a counter argument.

Writing Out Questions:
As you go through the evidence and the different phases, you should write down questions about the evidence that you wish to ask the students on the witness stand.

The more detailed and focused your questions, the more evidence you may be able to uncover. As well, by asking the correct questions, you may prove that some characters are lying or others are telling the truth. If you ask the wrong questions, you may not get enough information to either prosecute or defend the students. Make sure you are writing down any information that seems suspicious, or sometimes just asking to hear more about a story will give you a lead. The questions that you ask the students later in the trial will be vital to your case.

The Upper Crescent College Hockey Hazing Trial
Prosecution vs. Defense

K.J. Sukhu

Phase 2
The Bail Hearing

Now that the students have been formally charged, you must convince the Judge of their bail conditions. A bail hearing determines what restrictions will be applied to the Defendants while the trial proceeds. Common hearings may decide on a suspect's ability to travel or whether or not a curfew should be imposed (more possible bail conditions are listed on the next page). It will be important to "win" the bail hearing, as the outcome may affect future proceedings.

> *Note: Although it is important to "win" the bail hearing, be sure not to unveil too much of your evidence to the opposing side at this point. You don't want to give away your strategy and tactics.

The "winner" of this bail hearing will decide the outcome of the future of the UCC hockey season. The convener has stated, after working with investigators, that if players are allowed to resume all duties, then UCC will be permitted to continue their season. If any bail restrictions are imposed on the team that impact their ability to play, then UCC will be dropped for the season and relegated next year (once again this will impact future court proceedings).

PROSECUTION	DEFENSE
- Attempt to come up with bail conditions that restrict players' abilities to continue the season - Discuss your bail conditions with the Defense team before formally submitting your plan (try to reach a consensus)	- Attempt to come up with bail conditions that allow players to continue the season - Discuss your bail conditions with the Prosecution team before formally submitting your plan (try to reach a consensus)
- Submit a bail plan to your instructor (consensus or no consensus)	- Submit a bail plan to your instructor (consensus or no consensus)

The Upper Crescent College Hockey Hazing Trial
Prosecution vs. Defense

1. The Prosecution and Defense will decide upon a set of bail conditions separately (and give it to the instructor to look over).
    - This plan should include what conditions should be imposed (or not) and a reasonable explanation as to why (a possible list of conditions is located below).
    - Bail may be set for specific individuals or encompass all students charged (either decision is acceptable).

2. The Prosecution and Defense will then have some time to <u>discuss</u> their plans with each other. If a compromise can be worked out then you will hand in the agreed upon bail conditions to your instructor/judge.

    *Note: You may choose to show the other side some evidence to help further your argument but you do not have to. All you are obligated to do is discuss your bail conditions.

3. If a compromise cannot be reached then you will be given a chance to revise your plan prior to handing it in. Your instructor/judge will then rule on the specifics of the bail conditions given each side's explanations.

Bail Condition Examples	Description
Curfew	Should the defendants be allowed to leave their residence? If so, what hours should they be allowed to be out? Or, should there be no restrictions on the defendants?
Ability to go to School	Can students still attend school (and be able to interact)? Should students be homeschooled (so that they cannot interact)?
Ability to go to Work	Can students still attend their jobs (if they have one)?
Parental Supervision	Should parents alone be responsible for supervision or should defendants have to check in with an officer too?
Blood and Urine Test	Should the defendants be subjected to random blood and urine tests to make sure they are not abusing substances?
Driving Suspension	Should defendants be able to drive or should their licenses be suspended?
Remain in the Region	Should students be able to leave the area or should their passports be confiscated?
Money Paid to Court to Ensure Bail is upheld	How much money should defendants' families have to give the court (temporarily) to ensure they don't violate bail conditions?
People with Whom They may Interact	Are the defendants able/unable to interact with certain people?

*Note: You may do additional research or come up with creative bail conditions to present.

The Upper Crescent College Hockey Hazing Trial
Prosecution vs. Defense

Prosecution:
You want to limit the interaction among the defendants while not in court. You will attempt to convince the Judge that one (or more) of these scenarios may be more than likely:
- the accused may damage evidence that is vital to the case
- the accused may conspire to hide facts
- the accused are at risk of leaving the area while proceedings are taking place
- the accused may continue to carry on behavior that caused the alleged crime to occur

The Prosecution will be looking for the Judge to order:
1. Having the accused stay in juvenile hall or a detention centre while the proceedings are taking place.
2. Having the accused stay under a strict house arrest (curfew and terms should be outlined in your plan).
3. A restraining order among the accused.
4. That a large sum of money be provided as insurance for all bail conditions to be met, if bail is granted.

*Choose carefully and be realistic (you may have to compromise on some things). Remember to support your concerns with facts and evidence.

Defense:
You want life to remain normal for the students. That means that you want to avoid as many restrictions as possible. You must prove that the students have shown no indication that they would do any of the following:

- the accused may damage evidence that is vital to the case
- the accused may conspire to hide facts
- the accused are at risk of leaving the area while proceedings are taking place
- the accused may continue to carry on behavior that caused the alleged crime to occur

The Defense will be looking for the Judge to order:
1. No restrictions on the students.
2. If restrictions must be imposed, then the students will remain under a "limited" house arrest (curfew and terms should be outlined in your plan).
3. No restraining orders.
4. A small sum of money be handed over if bail is granted.

*Choose carefully and be realistic (you may have to compromise on some things).

For the bail conditions proposal submission, you may include as many restrictions as possible. The Defense should give evidence as to why they shouldn't be imposed and the prosecution should give evidence as to why conditions should be imposed. Be creative in the types of conditions and reasoning you give. If the opposing side is not ready for them, then it may become easier to win your terms when presented to your instructor/judge.

For your proposal you will need to fill in the chart on the following page just as the example below describes.

Example of bail conditions required to be submitted:

Bail Conditions	Applicable To:	Proposed Details	Reasoning
Curfew	Suspect X Suspect Y Suspect Z	Defendants are only permitted to leave their home from 8:30 am - 4:30 pm. No exceptions.	Suspects cannot be trusted beyond those hours because of evidence A, B, & C

Bail Conditions Proposal

Bail Conditions	Applicable To:	Proposed Details	Reasoning

The Upper Crescent College Hockey Hazing Trial
Prosecution vs. Defense

K.J. Sukhu

Bail Conditions	Applicable To:	Proposed Details	Reasoning

The Upper Crescent College Hockey Hazing Trial
Prosecution vs. Defense

K.J. Sukhu

Phase 3
Selecting people who will testify

Charges have been laid; bail has been set and the trial is about to begin. Before the trial can commence, the instructor/judge will need you to provide a list of people you wish to interview on the witness stand.

- Think carefully because the Judge may or may not allow you to add to this list later on.
- You will decide on the order in which to call your witnesses.
- You will be able to call any individuals from the team (including the coaches) to take the witness stand (with the exception being Mark Staffi).

*Note: The order you choose will be critical to gaining additional information. Think about who may be the most useful to you earlier on in the trial and who would be of more use to you later on. The order in which you call people might have an effect on their answers.

PROSECUTION	DEFENSE
- Prepare a list of questions you wish to ask the witnesses - Prepare opening statements	- Prepare a list of questions you wish to ask the witnesses - Prepare opening statements
- Submit a list of people you would like to put on the witness stand and the order in which they will testify	- Submit a list of people you would like to put on the witness stand and the order in which they will testify

Example:

Witness	Pertinent Information
1. Name	Witness X's story does not seem to line up with the facts. They are requested to take priority on the witness stand.
2.	

The Upper Crescent College Hockey Hazing Trial
Prosecution vs. Defense

K.J. Sukhu

Selecting the witnesses who will take the stand and their order:

Witness	Pertinent Information
1.	
2.	
3.	
4.	
6.	
7.	
8.	
9.	
10.	
11.	
12.	
13.	
14.	
15.	
16.	
17.	
18.	
19.	
20.	
21.	

The Upper Crescent College Hockey Hazing Trial
Prosecution vs. Defense

Phase 4
The trial can now begin

In the interest of time, the trial will proceed as follows:
1. Prosecution and Defense will read opening statements and what they wish to accomplish at the conclusion of the trial
2. The Prosecution will call their first witness and have a chance to ask questions.
3. The Defense will then have a chance to cross examine the witness (this counts as questioning the witness).
4. Next the Defense team will call a witness of their choosing.
5. The Prosecution will then have a chance to cross examine the witness.
6. This alternating pattern will continue until both sides no longer have witnesses to call upon.

*Note: The more specific you are with your questions and evidence the more helpful it will be to you case.

Alternatively, your Judge may change the format to have one side question all the characters first, and then allow the other side an opportunity for cross examination.

Trial Rules:
- Both sides will be able to ask the Judge for a 2 – 5 min recess in light of new information to revise their strategy (the Judge reserves the right to grant or deny their request).
- Neither the Defense nor the Prosecution can ask a witness to repeat an answer. It is up to that team to have a pencil and paper handy to record what is being said.

The Judge has the authority to change any rule they wish (it's their courtroom).

PROSECUTION	DEFENSE
- Examine each person's story and see if there are any discrepancies or additional information that may help your position	- Examine each person's story and see if there are any discrepancies or additional information that may help your position

When questioning the students, you should be prepared with a plan. Here are some useful tips to consider:
1. Go in with a strategy
   - Are you trying to prove that there is/isn't a history of violence?
   - Are you going to argue that the incident is/isn't severe?
   - Are you going to argue that there is/isn't enough evidence to convict the students?
   - Are there other hazing trials? What were the verdicts on those trials?

2. Have your questions prepared
   - Try and get students "on your side" to be convincing
   - Try to entrap students whose testimony may damage your case.

3. Be flexible
   - You may need to drop charges or add charges. Be ready to revise your tactics.
   - Write down everything that the students say (it's vital).

What should I expect when questioning the witnesses?
Some characters will lie and some will tell the truth. It's your job to review each statement and weave a logical story, so as to prove and disprove some characters' statements. Sometimes you will catch a suspect in a lie on the stand. At other times you will have to compare statements after the fact. Make sure you document what is being said and by whom. In your final report you will present your case and the statements that prove your case.

Be prepared for unexpected answers. You should anticipate what their responses should be, but, prepare a contingency plan in case they are not. If you are confronted with responses such as "I don't know" or "no comment", don't be discouraged. You may still use these comments to your advantage.

Phase 5
The conclusion

Examination of the witnesses has concluded. Now your "closing argument"/final write up can be given. Using the evidence, and the additional information gained from the witnesses, write out a logical account of the events that led to the injuries sustained by Mark Staffi.

Be sure to be specific in your report. This means:
1. Prove why suspects are either innocent or guilty (based on the evidence).
2. Discredit any character that disproves your case (backed up either by evidence or discrepancies revealed in the examination on the witness stand).
3. Substantiate any character that helps your case (backed up by evidence or information gained through the examination of the characters).
4. Establish the severity of the injury (by doing research on spinal injuries).
5. Cite other trials with similar outcomes.

Note to Prosecution: At this point it is wise to re-evaluate your strategy. You want to present the strongest case to the Judge. This means that you may have to drop the charges on any suspects for whom you have a lack of evidence. This may actually help Prosecute at least some of the members rather than losing the whole case.

Note to Defense: If there are members who you know are guilty, you may want to make a deal with the Prosecution. This way at least some of the students may walk away free.

PROSECUTION	DEFENSE
- Final write up	- Final write up

For your final report you will create a convincing argument as to which suspects should be charged or exonerated. Your report should include all your reasoning and logical explanations backed up by evidence and testimonial statements. The best argument will determine the fate of the characters.

Appendix

1. How to Cut DNA
2. What Does Mixed DNA Mean?
3. How to Analyze DNA

IMPORTANT: This report contains proprietary and original material. Accordingly, this document may not be copied or released to third parties without consent.

How to Cut DNA

In an assignment you were given the following information and told to figure out the bands of the DNA.
1. a Restriction Enzyme
2. a sample of DNA

1. Restriction Enzyme Fay-KE

CG
CG
TA
_____ Cut Here
AT
GC
GC

It is important to note that the DNA for the 6 strips should be considered one continuous strand. Meaning that "1" connects immediately to "2" and then to "3" and so on.

2. Sample of DNA

1	2	3	4	5	6
A-T	C-G	A-T	G-C	G-C	G-C
C-G	G-C	C-G	G-C	C-G	C-G
A-T	T-A	C-G	T-A	G-C	A-T
A-T	A-T	T-A	A-T	T-A	C-G
C-G	A-T	A-T	A-T	A-T	A-T
C-G	T-A	G-C	T-A	A-T	A-T
T-A	T-A	G-C	T-A	T-A	A-T
A-T	G-C	C-G	G-C	T-A	G-C
G-C	C-G	G-C	C-G	C-G	C-G
G-C	A-T	C-G	A-T	C-G	G-C
A-T	A-T	A-T	C-G	C-G	T-A
T-A	A-T	C-G	G-C	T-A	A-T
T-A	T-A	C-G	C-G	A-T	A-T
G-C	C-G	G-C	A-T	G-C	T-A
C-G	C-G	T-A	C-G	G-C	T-A
G-C	T-A	T-A	G-C	T-A	G-C
C-G	A-T	G-C	C-G	A-T	C-G
A-T	G-C	T-A	A-T	A-T	A-T
C-G	G-C	A-T	C-G	T-A	C-G

Step 1: Identify the areas that the restriction enzyme will cut (Figure A-1).

1	2	3	4	5	6
A-T	C-G	A-T	G-C	G-C	G-C
C-G	G-C	C-G	G-C	C-G	C-G
A-T	T-A	C-G	T-A	G-C	A-T
A-T	A-T	T-A	A-T	T-A	C-G
C-G	A-T	A-T	A-T	A-T	A-T
C-G	T-A	G-C	T-A	A-T	A-T
T-A	T-A	G-C	T-A	T-A	A-T
A-T	G-C	C-G	G-C	T-A	G-C
G-C	C-G	G-C	C-G	C-G	C-G
G-C	A-T	C-G	A-T	C-G	G-C
A-T	A-T	A-T	C-G	C-G	T-A
T-A	A-T	C-G	G-C	T-A	A-T
T-A	T-A	C-G	C-G	A-T	A-T
G-C	C-G	G-C	A-T	G-C	T-A
C-G	C-G	T-A	C-G	G-C	T-A
G-C	T-A	T-A	G-C	T-A	G-C
C-G	A-T	G-C	C-G	A-T	C-G
A-T	G-C	T-A	A-T	A-T	A-T
C-G	G-C	A-T	C-G	T-A	C-G

The restriction enzyme is very specific to and can only recognize one sequence. Any variation other than the one provided should not be counted.

For this example the DNA shows that the restriction enzyme Fay-KE appears a total of 4 times.

Figure A-1

Appendix   K.J. Sukhu

Step 2: Cut the DNA sequence specified by the restriction enzyme.

Figure A-2 shows the DNA "cut" using the restriction enzyme.

The DNA was cut 4 times.

    CG
    CG
    TA
——————— Cut Here
    AT
    GC
    GC

1	2	3	4	5	6
A-T	C-G	A-T	G-C	G-C	G-C
C-G	G-C	C-G	G-C	C-G	C-G
A-T	T-A	C-G	T-A	G-C	A-T
A-T	A-T	T-A	A-T	T-A	C-G
C-G	A-T	A-T	A-T	A-T	A-T
C-G	T-A	G-C	T-A	A-T	A-T
T-A	T-A	G-C	T-A	T-A	A-T
A-T	G-C	C-G	G-C	T-A	G-C
G-C	C-G	G-C	C-G	C-G	C-G
G-C	A-T	C-G	A-T	C-G	G-C
A-T	A-T	A-T	C-G	C-G	T-A
T-A	A-T	C-G	G-C	T-A	A-T
T-A	T-A	C-G	C-G	A-T	A-T
G-C	C-G	G-C	A-T	G-C	T-A
C-G	C-G	T-A	C-G	G-C	T-A
G-C	T-A	T-A	G-C	T-A	G-C
C-G	A-T	G-C	C-G	A-T	C-G
A-T	G-C	T-A	A-T	A-T	A-T
C-G	G-C	A-T	C-G	T-A	C-G

Figure A-2

Step 3: Identify the size of the fragments cut.

1	2	3	4	5	6
A-T	**C-G**	A-T	**G-C**	**G-C**	G-C
C-G	**G-C**	C-G	**G-C**	**C-G**	C-G
A-T	**T-A**	C-G	**T-A**	**G-C**	A-T
A-T	**A-T**	T-A	**A-T**	**T-A**	C-G
C-G	**A-T**	A-T	**A-T**	**A-T**	A-T
C-G	**T-A**	G-C	**T-A**	**A-T**	A-T
T-A	**T-A**	G-C	**T-A**	**T-A**	A-T
A-T	**G-C**	C-G	**G-C**	**T-A**	G-C
G-C	**C-G**	G-C	**C-G**	**C-G**	C-G
G-C	**A-T**	C-G	**A-T**	**C-G**	G-C
A-T	**A-T**	A-T	**C-G**	**C-G**	T-A
T-A	**A-T**	C-G	**G-C**	**T-A**	A-T
T-A	**T-A**	C-G	**C-G**	A-T	A-T
G-C	**C-G**	G-C	**A-T**	G-C	T-A
C-G	**C-G**	T-A	**C-G**	G-C	T-A
G-C	**T-A**	T-A	**G-C**	T-A	G-C
C-G	A-T	G-C	**C-G**	A-T	C-G
A-T	G-C	T-A	**A-T**	A-T	A-T
C-G	G-C	A-T	**C-G**	T-A	C-G

Since the DNA is considered continuous, by making 4 cuts, 5 DNA fragments have been created.

Figure A-3

Appendix

Step 4: Count the size of each fragment and make the bands on the gel electrophoreses.

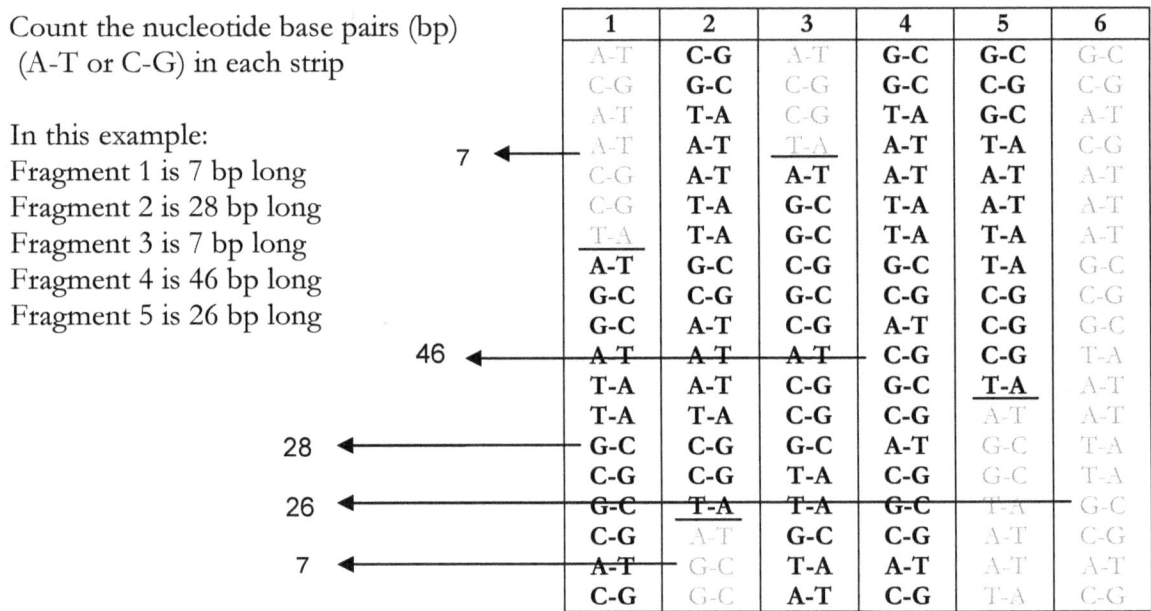

Count the nucleotide base pairs (bp) (A-T or C-G) in each strip

In this example:
Fragment 1 is 7 bp long
Fragment 2 is 28 bp long
Fragment 3 is 7 bp long
Fragment 4 is 46 bp long
Fragment 5 is 26 bp long

Figure A-4

Step 5: Place the bands on the gel.

Band	Mixed DNA
46	▭
28	▭
26	▭
7	▭

Figure A-5

The bands must be placed with the smallest fragments on the bottom and increasing in length as you go upwards.

You should also notice that single fragments such as band 26, 28 and 46 appear "thin", while bands that contain multiple fragments such as 7 appear "thick".

Once you have your bands identified as either a "thin" or "thick" band, you have completed sampling the DNA sequence for this particular character.

Note: Understanding the difference between "thin" bands and "thick" bands are only important to this assignment.

What Does Mixed DNA Mean?

During the case studies for Drewersville and The Dolphin you most likely encountered DNA such as the one pictured below.

Band	Mixed DNA
54	▭
44	▭
38	▭
33	▭
25	▭
24	▭
17	▭
12	▭
11	▭
10	▭
8	▭

Figure A-6

As the second column suggests this DNA sample contains mixed DNA. This means that the sample may contain more than one person's DNA. It could belong to victims, murderer(s), a close associate, or all of the above.

Use the DNA to place people at the scene of the crime. Remember, not all people may be a victim or murderer.

DNA is the key to placing a suspect at a crime scene. However, DNA alone will not solve the case; motive and evidence are also necessary.

How to Analyze DNA

At first you were given a DNA sequence (such as the picture shown to the right).

Let us say that this DNA belongs to suspect "X".

You've learned how to sequence this DNA in the previous section labeled "How to Cut DNA".

1	2	3	4	5	6
A-T	C-G	A-T	G-C	G-C	G-C
C-G	G-C	C-G	G-C	C-G	C-G
A-T	T-A	C-G	T-A	G-C	A-T
A-T	A-T	T-A	A-T	T-A	C-G
C-G	A-T	A-T	A-T	A-T	A-T
C-G	T-A	G-C	T-A	A-T	A-T
T-A	T-A	G-C	T-A	T-A	A-T
A-T	G-C	C-G	G-C	T-A	G-C
G-C	C-G	G-C	C-G	C-G	C-G
G-C	A-T	C-G	A-T	C-G	G-C
A-T	A-T	A-T	C-G	C-G	T-A
T-A	A-T	C-G	G-C	T-A	A-T
T-A	T-A	C-G	C-G	A-T	A-T
G-C	C-G	G-C	A-T	G-C	T-A
C-G	C-G	T-A	C-G	G-C	T-A
G-C	T-A	T-A	G-C	T-A	G-C
C-G	A-T	G-C	C-G	A-T	C-G
A-T	G-C	T-A	A-T	A-T	A-T
C-G	G-C	A-T	C-G	T-A	C-G

Figure A-7

Now that you have this DNA sequenced it appears as bands and numbers indicating the fragment size. Remember the "thick" bands contain multiple fragments of the same size. The "thin" bands contain only one fragment of that size.

Now you are ready to analyze the DNA found on the victims.

Band	Mixed DNA
46	☐
28	☐
26	☐
7	☐

Figure A-8

Let's compare the DNA that we sequenced belonging to Suspect "X" to a sample of DNA found on Victim "1" at a crime scene:

DNA found on Victim "1"   **Individual DNA of Suspect "X"**

Band	Mixed DNA
54	☐
44	☐
38	☐
33	☐
25	☐
24	☐
17	☐
12	☐
11	☐
10	☐
8	☐

Band	Mixed DNA
46	☐
28	☐
26	☐
7	☐

Figure A-9

When you compare the two you will notice that none of the bands that you sequenced from Suspect "X" match the DNA found on the victim's body. This means that Suspect "X" may not have been involved at the scene of this crime.

Appendix K.J. Sukhu

Let's now compare suspect Suspect "X's" DNA to a different sample found on Victim "2":

DNA found on Victim "2"   **Individual DNA of Suspect "X"**

Band	Mixed DNA
54	
46	
38	
33	
28	
26	
25	
17	
12	
11	
10	
7	

Band	Mixed DNA
46	
28	
26	
7	

Figure A-10

When comparing the suspect's DNA, all of his bands (bands 7, 26, 28 and 46) can be found on the victim's DNA. This means that suspect "X" must either be a murderer, a victim or has had a relationship with the victim. Only additional evidence can tell.

www.ingramcontent.com/pod-product-compliance
Lightning Source LLC
Chambersburg PA
CBHW080918170426
43201CB00016B/2190